WINGBEATS AND HEARTBEATS

WINGBEATS AND HEARTBEATS

Essays on
Game Birds, Gun Dogs, and Days Afield

DAVE BOOKS
Illustrated by CHRISTOPHER SMITH

THE UNIVERSITY OF WISCONSIN PRESS

The University of Wisconsin Press
1930 Monroe Street, 3rd Floor
Madison, Wisconsin 53711-2059
uwpress.wisc.edu

3 Henrietta Street
London WC2E 8LU, England
eurospanbookstore.com

Library of Congress Cataloging-in-Publication Data

Books, Dave.
Wingbeats and heartbeats: essays on game birds, gun dogs, and
days afield / Dave Books.
pages   cm
ISBN 978-0-299-29470-0 (cloth: alk. paper)
ISBN 978-0-299-29473-1 (e-book)
1. Fowling—United States—Anecdotes.
2. Game and game-birds—United States—Anecdotes.
3. Hunting dogs—United States—Anecdotes.   I. Title.
SK313.B693   2014
799.2′4—dc23
2013015043

First, this book is dedicated to
HELEN and LES, my parents,
who taught me to love and cherish the outdoors.

Next, to
the gun dogs who have made my days afield so rewarding:
BULLET, CHIEF, MAGGIE, SALLY, GROUCHO,
JENNY, OLLIE, and BAILEY.

Finally, to
ALL MY HUNTING BUDDIES,
who have made it so much fun. If I start naming names I might
forget someone, but you know who you are.

Contents

Contents

Contents

Acknowledgments

Some of these stories, or earlier versions of them, have appeared in hunting and conservation magazines, notably *Pheasants Forever, Quail Forever, Ducks Unlimited, Ruffed Grouse Society Magazine, Montana Outdoors, Gun Dog, Wing & Shot, Under Wild Skies*, and *The Upland Almanac*. I'd like to thank the editors of these magazines for their help and encouragement, especially Mark Herwig, Matt Young, Tom Dickson, Chuck Wechsler, and Tom Carney.

Introduction

It's late August, and the nights have been getting noticeably cooler here in the Rocky Mountain foothills. The cold rain that began stitching down this morning has been drumming a steady cadence on the cedar shingles all day long. That's how summer ends in Montana. One day it's blistering hot and you're wading a trout stream in shorts and a T-shirt; the next day dawns cold and rainy, with a fresh-off-a-glacier wind. Tomorrow, wet snow will likely blanket the high country. It's time to say goodbye to summer and get ready for the opening of upland bird season on September 1.

The dogs, too, sense the change. When I took them for a walk in the rain this morning, Ollie the Brittany, a veteran of nine hunting seasons, bounced around like a six-month-old pup. Bailey, a four-year-old black Lab who loves the snow and cold, twirled in excited circles, free at last of summer's oppressive heat. Her excitement is premature, of course, because when this storm passes there will be plenty of warm September days, followed by the glorious Indian summer days of October. But this first autumn storm will chase the tourists back to more hospitable climes, muttering, "Winter sure comes early in Montana."

For the last three decades I've opened the bird season somewhere in Montana, always with a Lab or a Brittany, and usually both. Before that, with the exception of a few college years, I spent opening days chasing ruffed grouse and woodcock in Wisconsin, Minnesota, or Upper Michigan. Thanks to a father who introduced me to the Wisconsin grouse woods before I was old enough to carry a gun, I've been in love with game birds and shotguns since childhood. My life has been richer for it, if not my pocketbook.

One day not long ago, while I was rattling on about bird hunting to an acquaintance, he said, "You're really *passionate* about it, aren't you?" I hadn't thought of my favorite pastime that way, but I had to admit he was right. I enjoy a lot of outdoor activities—fishing, hiking, birding, camping, wildlife photography—but wingshooting is in my blood.

What is it about bird hunting that compels us to spend countless hours training dogs and logging hundreds—or even thousands—of miles every fall in search of a perfect hunt? In part, it's the wildness and beauty of the birds themselves. Upland game birds and waterfowl are noble creatures, the product of healthy habitats in rural landscapes. Whether it's a long-spurred rooster pheasant in a Montana river bottom or a diminutive Gambel's quail in Arizona's Sonoran desert, game birds in flight against an autumn sky are the stuff of hunters' dreams.

But it's more than just the birds we seek. It's the peace and serenity of the places where game birds live. It's the fragrance of decaying leaves, the sight of hardwoods ablaze with color, the rose-tinged beauty of a prairie sunrise, the tang of autumn in the air. It's the elegance and athleticism of gun dogs, doing what they've been bred and trained to do. It's the heft of a familiar shotgun, perhaps one handed down from a father or grandfather. It's the freedom to walk the woods or prairies until your legs ache, and come home happy at the end of the day. It's the priceless hours spent afield with friends and family. It's the bird hunter's road—hunting rigs, leaky tents, campfires, small-town cafés, and mom-and-pop motels where the signs say "Hunters Welcome."

There are many ways to enjoy bird hunting, but the one I have chosen is simple: no fancy hunting lodges with planted birds, no quail plantations with mule-drawn wagons, no driven birds in England or Scotland, no sizzling dove shoots in South America. I have nothing against these things; they're fine for hunters with the financial means and the inclination to enjoy them. But for me, it has always been wild birds, a dog I've trained from a pup, an old gun that has served me well, and plenty of boot leather. Most of the time, my hunting trips have not yielded a bulging game bag. But they've provided me something more valuable: a wealth of experience, a slew of adventures, and a rich storehouse of memories. In the end, it's not how many birds you shoot that is important; it's how you take them and how you honor their taking.

Because I respect and admire gun dogs—both the upland breeds and waterfowl retrievers—you'll read much about them here. For me, following gun dogs has been an irresistible calling, and I've been fortunate to roam the fields and marshes with several fine ones. More important, my dogs have shared and enriched my life year-round, and for that I owe them much. I hope you'll enjoy coming along with us in the pages of this book.

UPLAND TALES

All the birds are noble. All are wild, and hunting them is the one way I know to get closest to them.

Charles Fergus, A Rough-Shooting Dog

Autumn Magic

I suppose I was eight or nine when Dad and Uncle Hal gave in to my pleading and let me tag along on one of their Saturday ruffed grouse hunts. Of course, my dad and uncle didn't call these birds "ruffed grouse," nor did anyone else in the west-central Wisconsin of my youth. To us they were simply "partridge."

So, on a bright October morning, with the hardwoods decked out in their autumn finest, I laced up my new leather boots and went, unarmed, on my first partridge hunt. Before we entered the woods Dad issued my marching orders: "Keep quiet, stay right behind me and stop when I stop." I was happy to comply. Going hunting was heady stuff for a kid my age.

Dad and Uncle Hal were dogless hunters in those days. They had grown up in a large family on a hardscrabble Dunn County farm, and bird dogs had not been part of their heritage. But as boys they had spent plenty of time in the woods pursuing partridge, rabbits, and squirrels. They knew how to hunt.

It wasn't long before my feet began to get cold, but I was determined not to complain. Dad and Uncle Hal moved quietly through the woods, always keeping each other within sight and sound. They stopped often, which puzzled me at the time. They certainly couldn't be tired; the more we stood still, the colder my feet became. Later, Dad explained, "A partridge gets nervous when you stop walking. That's when he's most likely to flush."

On one of our stop-and-listen sessions, a bird did just that. Its thunderous takeoff nearly made me jump out of my new boots. It bored straightaway, and a second later Dad's "Sweet 16" Browning humpback roared. The bird cartwheeled down and I raced after it, forgetting Dad's warning to stay behind him. Luckily for me, no other birds took wing. If they had, Dad might have benched me for the year.

The grouse's wings were still fluttering when I got there, making it easy to find. I gazed down at the most beautiful creature I had ever seen. Taking off my wool mittens, I picked the bird up and ran my fingers over its warm body, stroking the silky black ruff, mottled brown back and banded tail. For a moment, the grouse and I were alone in a wild sanctuary, a mystical world of golden tamaracks, purple dogwoods, and crimson swamp maples, where the pleasant aroma of decaying ferns permeated the air.

Footsteps crunching in the fallen leaves snapped me out of my reverie. "He marks the fall as well as most bird dogs," said Uncle Hal, "but he's a little slow on the fetching part."

Dad laughed and put his hand on my shoulder. "Yep, it looks like we've got us a hunting partner." I didn't know it at the time, but that childhood encounter with the king of game birds changed my life. It marked the beginning of a long love affair with autumn, upland birds, shotguns, and eventually bird dogs.

The next autumn, Dad let me carry an unloaded gun—a Winchester Model 1890 pump-action .22, complete with octagon barrel and peep sight. When anyone in our party spotted a squirrel, I was allowed to load the gun. That sweet little rifle, handed down for generations, accounted for a lot of bushytails. I still have it today.

I'm sure I received some nice gifts on my twelfth birthday, but the only one I remember came in a long, heavy box. Heart racing, I tore open the package to find my first shotgun, a 16 gauge Ithaca Model 37 Featherlight pump. From then on, I would hunt partridge with Dad, Uncle Hal, and Hal's son-in-law, Jack.

Had I known how many birds I would miss during those early years, I may have opted for a different sport. I was small for my age and the gun was stocked for a grown man. It had a modified choke, a bit on the tight side for grouse in close quarters. Dad was a thrifty man and he deemed shortening the stock a waste of good walnut, allowing that I'd "grow into it." Burning up shells on clay pigeons was likewise considered a waste of time and money. He figured I'd learn to shoot as he had, by trial and error.

In my case there was plenty of error. Partridge were abundant, and the grouse cycle, of which I knew nothing at the time, must have been at its peak. I sometimes started out with a box of shells and returned at the end of the day, birdless and dejected, with only a few shells left. About when I had given up all hope of ever hitting a bird on the wing, a grouse roared out of a dogwood thicket and angled left. Although my track record suggested I should save my ammunition, I mounted the gun, swung and fired. When the bird tumbled to the ground I let out a yell that brought my father on the run. I'm not sure who was happier, Dad or I. Maybe he was just relieved that I hadn't shot myself in the foot.

As I grew bigger the gun began to fit me better, and I began knocking down a bird here and there. College came along and didn't allow much time for hunting. But in forestry school at the University of Minnesota I met Rod Sando, a husky, crew-cut farm kid from a small town north of the Twin Cities. A few years after graduation we both landed jobs with the research branch of the U.S. Forest Service in St. Paul and began hunting together.

It didn't take me long to find out that Rod was the most skillful ruffed grouse hunter I had ever seen. He had laser eyesight and fast reflexes, but more important, he had grown up prowling the woods around his family farm. He seemed to know what the grouse were going to do before they knew it themselves. He also had a dog with a great nose, a yellow Lab named Punch.

Rod had a Remington Model 870 pump with a full choke, not exactly a grouse hunter's dream gun. But even with that full choke, Rod was a deadly shot, especially later in the fall. Many times I saw him shoot through the leafless branches to bring down a grouse at more than forty yards.

In his classic book, *New England Grouse Shooting*, William Harnden Foster asserts that the ablest of the old New England market hunters often shot 300 or more grouse in a single season. "The old timers who were shooting pa'tridges for a business," wrote Foster,

"hunted practically every day for three months and some of them stretched the season a bit at that." I have no doubt that Rod and Punch, hunting as many days, could have held their own with those old boys and their dogs.

I asked Rod for advice on how to cure my shooting woes. He said, "Get a Remington 870 like mine with a full choke." Not surprisingly, that gun didn't make me a better grouse shot. In fact, it made me worse, although on waterfowl and long-range pheasants it sometimes did me proud.

My epiphany came when I visited a skeet range for the first time. The manager watched me struggle through a round of skeet with my full-choke gun, breaking only ten or twelve targets, and took pity on me. He handed me a beat-up Browning over/under choked skeet and skeet, and said, "Here, try this." I broke nineteen birds with it on my first round and twenty-one on the next. He then gave me a lecture on the importance of choke in shotguns, but he needn't have. I already had my mind set on buying a new gun.

I moved to Montana not long after, and didn't see Rod for several years. When we eventually got together again for a ruffed grouse hunt in Minnesota, a number of things had changed. Rod had traded his Remington Model 870 for a sleek little over/under choked skeet and skeet. Punch had passed on and Rod now had an English setter named Lars.

I had shelved my full-choke Remington in favor of a Browning over/under choked improved cylinder and modified, a good combination for Montana's more open conditions, and I had a young Brittany named Chief. Smoking hundreds of clays at the trap and skeet club in Missoula had boosted my confidence.

Rod and I each shot several grouse over our dogs on that trip but the one I remember best came at the end of the last day. We were headed down a tote road on our way back to the truck when Lars stiffened on point at the edge of the trail. Chief was right behind him, backing. Rod motioned for me to walk in, figuring I'd miss, just like the old days, and he'd still have time to knock down the bird. I didn't miss. He slapped me on the back and said, "You've been practicing, haven't you?" I admitted that I had, but I couldn't help reminding him that he'd set back my learning curve by several years when he advised me to buy that Remington pump with the full choke.

Although five decades of wingshooting have taken me from Canada to the Mexican border, I have special memories of Wisconsin, where the noble ruffed grouse reigns. Chief was getting on in years by the time we headed east to revisit the grouse woods I had hunted with my dad and uncle as a boy. We arrived at the Flambeau River early one October morning, just as the sun began to light the treetops with crimson, orange, and yellow. I poured the last cup of coffee from the thermos and relaxed as the melting frost unlocked the sweet, damp smell of decomposing hardwood leaves. Uncasing my Browning, I slipped a dozen shells in the pockets of my hunting vest and buckled a Swiss bell on Chief's collar.

We'd hunted the better part of an hour when Chief's bell fell silent near the river, under the alder trees. I circled toward the riverbank, thinking the bird might be pinned near the water's edge. I had a clear shot when it topped the alders, and I heard it hit the ground with a thump. Chief came back a minute later with the ruffed grouse in his mouth.

I sat for a time on a pine log near the river, enjoying the sun on my face and smoothing the bird's feathers, admiring its beautiful plumage, just as I had so long ago on that first hunting trip with my father. A gray squirrel chattered on a far-off hardwood ridge; the dark waters of the Flambeau glided along, murmuring their secrets of grouse and deer and wild places they'd been. When I shut my eyes and listened, I could hear the voices of old hunting pals calling Ruff, Rosie, or Sophie—ghost dogs whose names I hadn't heard in years.

For those of us who appreciate tradition—and most wingshooters do—it's comforting to know things haven't changed too much in the grouse woods. Bird numbers ebb and flow, according to the vagaries of weather, habitat, and cyclic forces not completely understood. We now have modern conveniences like GPS units, Gore-Tex boots, and beeper collars, but the time-honored trinity of shotgun, bird, and dog remains. Wingbeats and heartbeats still collide at the crucial moment of the flush, just as they did for our fathers and grandfathers. Today's grouse hunters find freedom and adventure, and on occasion, magic, just like the hunters of generations past.

Completing the Picture

———◦⟨❦⟩◦———

Brittanys and woodcock seem to belong together, perhaps because they knew each other back in France, the ancestral home of the little "poacher's dog." In France, where the woodcock is known as the *becasse*, he is still hunted with Brittanys, French griffons, and other pointing breeds. The Club National des Becassiers (French Woodcock Society) imposes strict rules for hunting *Scolopax rusticola*, the European woodcock. Members shoot birds only over points, and their dogs wear bells—no electronic gadgets allowed. The European bird closely resembles our American woodcock, *Scolopax minor*, except in size. *Scolopax rusticola* is a woodcock on steroids, weighing in at about twelve ounces, roughly twice the size of our bird.

I have a Robert Abbett painting of a hunting scene that evokes a nostalgic, "I've been there" feeling. Entitled *Late Day Woodcock*, it features a forest of birches and other hardwoods with a languid brook running through it. In the painting, a Brittany stands at the edge of the water gazing up at a just-flushed woodcock, while his master takes aim with a vintage shotgun. Golden leaves litter the water and the tableau is suffused in soft afternoon light. I guess Abbett could have chosen a setter or another pointing breed, but somehow the Brittany seems to fit just right.

I wish I could say my earliest recollections of woodcock hunting resembled the scene in the painting, but they don't. In my first few years of wingshooting, we didn't have a dog. But that didn't keep us from blazing away when we bumped an occasional 'doodle while grouse hunting. Then one day Dad brought home a Brittany pup, a little male we christened Rufus. Dad and I had high hopes of becoming gentlemen woodcock hunters, just like members of the French Woodcock Society.

There was only one small problem. We knew nothing about training a bird dog. Our method consisted of taking Rufus hunting when he got big enough and hoping for the best. Not surprisingly, Rufus didn't point many birds the first fall. Wild as a hawk, he ran through the Wisconsin woods like Usain Bolt in an Olympic sprint, scattering birds, rabbits, squirrels, and anything else in his path. One day he pointed a feral cat, which we considered a good omen.

On our last hunt of the year Rufus barreled out of the woods into one of the narrow dirt roads we called fire lanes just as two hunters in a station wagon were driving by. It wasn't clear whether Rufus collided with the car or vice versa, but Rufus tumbled like a ground-sluiced grouse. The hunters bailed out of their car while Dad and I hurried to the scene. For a moment we all stood in silence, looking down at the motionless dog. "Jeez," said the crestfallen driver, "I'm sorry. I didn't see him until it was too late."

Dad took the high road. "It's not your fault. There's nothing you could have done." I could feel angry tears welling up in my eyes, but I knew it was the truth. Then Rufus twitched. A few seconds later, he lurched to his feet with a glazed look in his eyes. Hackles raised, he wobbled toward the metal beast that had knocked him down and began to bark and growl. Rufus made a full recovery, although from that point on whenever he did something goofy—which was often—we blamed it on his accident.

By the time Rufus turned three he had become a useful hunting dog, if not a model of bird-handling perfection. He pointed several grouse and pheasants that year and retrieved most of the birds we shot. But he saved his best performances for woodcock.

One mid-October day Dad and I stumbled onto an abandoned pasture grown up with young birch and popple. The ground cover looked a bit too open for grouse, and we almost passed it by. Luckily we didn't, because the pasture was stiff with migrating woodcock. Rufus trundled from one bug-eyed point to another, his progress interrupted only by bringing in our birds.

The next year I went off to college, and my hunting days were limited. But book learning, too, has its rewards. A forestry student at the University of Minnesota, I spent a spring quarter at the Cloquet Forestry Center near Duluth. My classmates and I lived in cabins, ate in a communal mess hall, and took classes, most of which involved fieldwork. The high point for me was a wildlife biology course taught by Gordon Gullion, who went on to fame as a ruffed grouse researcher and author of a book called *Grouse of the North Shore*. Dr. Gullion introduced us to the private lives of the ruffed grouse and woodcock, both residents of the Cloquet Experimental Forest.

I have two vivid memories of Dr. Gullion's biology class. Because most of our courses required working in the woods, we were issued hard hats for safety reasons. Dr. Gullion reminded us to wear them, since it was goshawk nesting season and goshawks are fierce protectors of their nests. Gordon was quite bald, and one day he showed up in class with a large bandage on his head. He'd forgotten his hard hat and paid the price.

The other was our visit to a woodcock singing ground to watch the bird's spectacular mating display, a performance Aldo Leopold called the "sky dance." Hidden at the edge of a clearing, we waited, shivering, as the early-April sun slid toward the western horizon. Somewhere in the distance a ruffed grouse drummed, sounding like a vintage tractor starting up. Just as we began to wonder if Dr. Gullion had taken us on an old-fashioned snipe hunt, a long-billed apparition fluttered into the clearing and landed.

Cold hands and feet forgotten, we watched as he strutted back and forth, emitting the nasal buzz Dr. Gullion referred to as a *peent*. Suddenly the bird flushed, flying low at first, then spiraling up, higher and higher, until he was a speck against the pink evening sky. He hovered briefly, then poured forth a liquid warble, a song he repeated several times as he zigzagged back to earth. Over the next half-hour, as the sky grew darker, he made six more courtship flights.

After watching for a time we quietly withdrew, leaving the 'doodle to his romantic endeavors. At some point, said Dr. Gullion, perhaps just at dark, a hen would fly in to join him on his singing ground and they would mate.

We learned that woodcock hens lay four (rarely five) large, cinnamon-colored eggs in a nest on the ground and incubate them for twenty-one days. Woodcock chicks, like those of ruffed grouse, are precocious; within a few hours of hatching they are ready to travel. A few days later the hen and her chicks may be some distance from the nest, busily foraging for worms and bugs. In another month they are almost full grown and able to fly.

Some time after I left the Midwest and moved west, I began to miss my little friend the timberdoodle. It wasn't for lack of bird hunting opportunities, since Montana has five species of grouse as well as pheasants and Hungarian partridge. But there are no woodcock. The Robert Abbett painting hanging in my den kept reminding me that my Octobers were lacking something.

One summer evening I called my cousin, Emil, who has a farm in central Wisconsin, where a purling, tea-colored stream wanders among the hardwoods. After we'd caught up on family news I got to the point. "Do you ever see any woodcock in that alder patch down by the creek?"

"Sure," he said, "sometimes there's a bunch of 'em there in the fall. But it seems like they're here one day and gone the next."

That was all I needed to hear. "Any chance I could come out with my dog in October and look around?"

"Just give me a call when you get here," he said.

A few months later I walked across Emil's pasture and entered the streamside alders with my Brittany, Chief. When I saw the white splotches dappling the fallen leaves and dark humus—woodcock "chalk"—I couldn't help but smile. At least one 'doodle had stopped here, maybe more. Before we'd gone far, Chief stopped near a clump of alders and stared at the ground. When I took a step forward a woodcock flushed, twisting and twittering upward through the branches. At the height of his climb my load of No. 8 shot brought him back to earth.

Chief looked perplexed when he brought me the 'doodle, as if to ask, "Are you sure you want these funny little birds?" I made a fuss over him to let him know I did indeed want those funny little birds.

Like Rufus had done so many years before, he pointed one woodcock after another that day.

Back home in Montana, I saw my Robert Abbett painting in a whole new light. After years of wishful thinking, I'd finally painted myself into the scene. *Vive la becasse!*

Humbled by Huns

I eased around the corner of the abandoned ranch house and squinted into the warm October sun. My gaze swept quickly over the rusting farm machinery and the dilapidated stable. Except for a light breeze rustling the golden leaves of a cottonwood, things were quiet—too quiet. I felt like I was about to become part of the shootout at the O.K. Corral.

Then I saw what I was looking for—my Brittany, Chief, frozen on point in the brown weeds next to an old hay rake. I didn't know whether to expect a covey of Hungarian partridge, a rattlesnake, or Wyatt Earp. Tightening my grip on the worn checkering of the Browning over/under, I slid my thumb against the safety. As I walked past the dog's rigid form, out of the corner of my eye I could see his pink nostrils monitoring the scent emanating from the grass. "Okay, Mr. Pink Nose, what have you got this time?" I wondered.

No matter how ready you are for the whir of those stubby wings, you're never *really* ready. Just as I began to suspect the birds had moved, they exploded from the grass, chirping like a dozen rusty gates in a prairie windstorm. I regained my composure in time to sort one bird out of the blur and stick with it until the sight picture looked right. The bird folded just as the covey veered out of sight around the corner of the stable.

Chief fetched the handsome gray-brown Hun, and I slipped it in my game vest. I hadn't been able to see where the covey had gone, but I guessed they would head for the old corral about 300 yards away. Coveys in past years had flown to this collection of rusty barbed wire, boards, tall grass, and weeds. I'd try to find them one more time, then, win or lose, I'd leave them for another day.

After you get to know a covey well enough, you begin to take a personal interest in it. As a hunter, you want to shoot your share of birds, but you also want to leave the covey strong enough to withstand the depredations of foxes, hawks, and winter storms. You know that one evening next spring you'll drive out to the old homestead to watch and listen, worrying a little until you hear the raspy love song of a mating pair. But now it's hunting season, and you're sure this covey is more than capable of coping with old Pink Nose and his jangle-nerved sidekick.

As much as Hungarian partridge seem to belong on the prairies of western North America, they're not native to the region. Their natural home is Europe, the British Isles, the Scandinavian countries, and parts of Asia, where they are better known as gray partridge. We call them Hungarians because that is where most of our imported birds came from. Huns were released in various locations in the eastern U.S. throughout the 1800s, but the climate and terrain weren't suitable and those early introductions didn't take. It wasn't until the early 1900s, when Huns were stocked in the wheat belt region of eastern Washington and Oregon, southern Alberta, Montana, and North Dakota, that things began to pop. Maybe "explode" is a better word, since the Hun quickly demonstrated the reproductive capacity that has made it a mainstay of European upland shooting for hundreds of years.

The most spectacular of the western plantings took place in southern Alberta in 1908 and 1909. With the support of a wealthy Michigan bird hunter named William Mershon, a group of Calgary sportsmen released 800 partridge near Calgary. Within five years these birds had multiplied and spread across southern Alberta and into Saskatchewan and Montana. Aldo Leopold later calculated their rate of spread at twenty-eight miles per year.

So successful was the expansion of Huns from the Calgary planting that by the mid-1930s outdoor author Ray Holland could report flushing more than a hundred separate coveys in a day's outing on the Saskatchewan prairie. Not bad, considering the province of Saskatchewan had not stocked a single bird! Those spectacular populations of the 1930s eventually crashed, but not before the Hun had established itself as a game bird throughout the prairie provinces and wheat country of the Northwest.

Today, southern Alberta and Saskatchewan remain the heart of the Hun range, but Montana, North Dakota, Idaho, and eastern Washington and Oregon also support good numbers. Other states with limited but huntable populations include Nevada, Utah, Wyoming, South Dakota, Minnesota, Wisconsin, and Iowa. Like other upland game birds, Huns are subject to cycles of abundance and scarcity. Although Huns get along better with modern agriculture than most game birds, they too are hurt by horizon-to-horizon plowing. Even in the best Hun country, Ray Holland's hundred-covey days are a thing of the past.

Hun coveys, which consist of a mating pair, their offspring, and other adults unsuccessful at mating, contain ten to twenty birds. Hun populations have a 75 percent turnover each year, so a three- or four-year-old bird is an old-timer. Coveys occupy the same favored sites year after year; in good years there may be several coveys in a given locale, while in lean years the population may shrink to a single covey.

Although Huns do best in wheat country where waste grain is available in fall and winter, they don't need it to survive. One fall, while hunting an uncultivated area along the Snake River in Idaho, two friends and I ran across an incredibly high density of Huns. We had been chukar hunting, climbing the rocky slopes above the river for most of the day without much luck. Toward late afternoon we dropped down to the grassy benches just above the river and stumbled into the best Hun shooting any of us had seen.

In agricultural areas, hunters will do best by checking the edges of stubble fields in morning and late afternoon when the birds are feeding. During the middle of the day, abandoned homesteads, brushy draws between grain fields, and weed patches are likely to produce birds. Huns favor light cover over thick undergrowth, and I've even flushed them from plowed fields where they were as invisible squatting in the dark soil as if they had been hunkered down in knee-high bunchgrass.

One time Mike Gurnett and I watched a covey sail into a small patch of weeds and grass surrounded by alternating strips of wheat stubble and fallow field. Licking our chops, we quickly covered the 200 yards to the little island of cover. We combed every inch of it— twice. As we stood there scratching our heads, Mike asked, "Where the heck did they go?" Just then the birds flushed from the bare field in front of us, leaving us so rattled we didn't fire a shot.

For a long time the Hun in America didn't get the credit it deserves for being a first-rate game bird. For one thing, it has always lived in the shadow of its showier fellow-immigrant, the ring-necked pheasant. Then, too, there is the nature of the places where most Huns live: big, open country, thinly populated with humans. Local folks may sing the Hun's praises, but perhaps there aren't enough voices out there to be heard above the yipping of lonely coyotes.

Good quail or ruffed grouse shots who visit the prairie often wonder how they can miss Huns, where there are few trees to obstruct their view. But Huns often flush farther out than the birds they're accustomed to, and snap shooting techniques don't work well. With Huns the first shot is often about twenty-five yards, and the second may be thirty-five or forty. Once newcomers adjust to the longer distances and stronger follow-through required, they score better. This is not to say that Huns are tougher targets than quail or vice versa—just different. Wingshooters become programmed for the birds they hunt most often, and it takes time to adjust to something new.

The best Hun shooters are the smooth ones who don't rush things and who swing through their birds strongly but deliberately. Hurrying to put lead in the air is a common mistake, and when I

hear someone rattle off a string of shots I don't expect many casualties. With Huns there is rarely time for more than two careful shots, and a shot at a fourteen-ounce bird at thirty-five yards has to be right on target. I hear sport shop talk about triples on Huns, but honest triples (taking three birds on a covey rise) are about as common as neck shots on running antelope.

One thing that complicates Hun shooting is the everlasting prairie wind. When it kicks up its heels, strange things happen to the flight patterns of birds. Duck hunters will understand. I once flushed a Hun into the teeth of a strong wind, and as I watched it over my gun barrel it began to look bigger instead of smaller. Suddenly it tired of bucking the wind, turned, and came directly toward me, buzzing over my head like a feathered bullet. I didn't get that one.

Huns can be humbling. I remember a blustery day when my partners, hunting some distance away, flushed a covey in my direction. I enjoy pass shooting and relished the chance to show off in front of an audience. But these Huns were different—they came at me like shrapnel out of a gunmetal sky, scattered, flying high and riding the galloping wind. I missed with both barrels, and went on to miss several easier shots after that. So much for overconfidence.

Despite their small size, Huns are tough birds. Many times I've watched one fly 100 yards or more before succumbing to a pellet or two in the body cavity. For that reason, I try to watch the covey as long as I can see it, even if I think I've missed. A bird that drops straight down out of such a covey often will be dead, while a bird that appears to be flying normally but lands short of the others may be wounded.

It goes without saying that dogs are a great help in hunting Huns. There is a lot of country to swallow up the birds, and a wide-ranging pointing dog will find more Huns than a close-working flusher. But any good dog is helpful, especially when it comes to finding and retrieving downed birds.

In recent years more hunters have discovered the pleasures of hunting Huns on the northern plains with pointing dogs. Conditions are best in early fall, but I've had memorable hunts later in the year. One crisp November day my Brittany, Ollie, made a wide cast into the wheat stubble adjacent to the Conservation Reserve field we had been hunting. When he topped a rise and disappeared, I didn't follow; it was late afternoon and I was bone-tired. Besides, I figured he'd be back in a minute or two. After five minutes had elapsed, I trudged to the top of the hill to investigate.

When I topped the hill I beheld a sight guaranteed to warm the heart of any wingshooter and give exhausted legs a sudden shot of adrenaline: A hundred yards below, Ollie stood motionless, head high, pointing toward an island of stunted brown weeds in the ocean of wheat stubble. I hurried ahead, expecting a nervous covey to take flight any second. As I closed the distance, my mood ricocheted from doubt to hopefulness to guarded optimism: fifty yards, twenty yards . . . ten yards . . . five yards . . . suddenly a covey of Huns lifted skyward in a flurry of wings. I dropped a bird with the improved cylinder barrel of my over/under, then swung well ahead of the last bird in the covey and downed it with the modified choke. Ollie retrieved both birds to hand, transforming a long, luckless afternoon into an instant success.

As we headed for the truck, the sinking sun peeked from beneath a gray cloudbank, casting an orange glow across the landscape. In the distance, the reedy calls of the scattered Huns drifted to us on the breeze—the familiar sound of a covey gathering for the night.

Snowbelly

———⟨⟩———

Cocking a quizzical eyebrow over a squinched-down blue eye, the old rancher sputtered, "Sharp-tailed *what*?"

"Sharp-tailed grouse, you know, the brown prairie birds with the pointed . . ."

"Oh, you mean *chickens*!" he interrupted. "Why didn't you say so in the first place?"

Had I known Ed a little better, I would have noticed the beginnings of a smile lurking under his bushy gray mustache and the mischievous twinkle in his eyes. Ed, who ranches in the rolling grassland country south of Malta, Montana, knew full well what sharp-tailed grouse were, but, like most Montana ranchers, he's always called them "chickens." Since I was a stranger in his country, he figured I should learn to speak his language.

When my hunting prospects are hanging in the balance, I learn quickly. "Any chance I could do some, uh, chicken hunting on your place tomorrow?" I asked.

"Suppose so," he said, "provided you're willin' to park your truck and walk."

Just then the soft winnowing of wings sounded above us, and we looked up to see a squadron of sharptails flying high and fast, white undersides flashing silver in the fading light, headed for some distant roosting place. "Pretty, ain't they?" Ed said, as we watched them grow smaller and finally disappear into the rose-tinged prairie sunset. "Should call 'em snowbellies."

The handsome, homespun sharptail is closely intertwined with the human and natural history of the northern plains. Native American dancers mimicked the sharptail's elaborate courtship ritual and used its feathers for decoration. Lewis and Clark observed large numbers of the "pointed tail prairie hen" on their journey up the Missouri, and were impressed with the birds' specialized means of coping with northern winters: "The toes are also curiously bordered on their lower edges with narrow hard scales . . . thus adding to the width of the tread which nature seems . . . to have furnished them at this season for passing over the snow with more ease."

The sharptail later greeted the pioneer cattlemen, whose herds replaced the bison on the western plains. Teddy Roosevelt, who ranched near the North Dakota–Montana border in the 1880s, wrote: "On more than one occasion I would have gone supperless or dinnerless had it not been for some of these grouse. . . . By the middle of August the young are well enough grown to shoot, and are then most delicious eating."

Market hunters, too, took advantage of the sharptail's table qualities. Setting out in the morning with a horse-drawn buckboard, they would return with a wagonload of birds to be barreled and shipped to eastern cities. In 1879, the Grand Pacific Hotel in Chicago included "roast pin-tail grouse" among a long list of game delicacies.

In the late 1800s and early 1900s the sharptail helped feed the army of homesteaders flocking to Dakota and Montana territories, lured by the promise of free land and a new beginning. With fresh meat often in short supply, they welcomed the addition of "chickens" to the family larder. In M. D. Johnson's book, *Feathers from the Prairie*, one old-timer reminisced on life in the 1890s: "We generally ate one or two [sharptails] whenever we wanted them at any time of the year. It was common for nearly everyone to live off grouse in those days."

Poking around the abandoned homesteads that dot the eastern Montana prairie, one can almost feel the presence of the hardy souls who lived there. Most reaped a bitter harvest of dust and despair, but some—perhaps the toughest or the luckiest—endured droughts, blizzards, grasshoppers, and hailstorms to carve out a permanent niche on the prairie. Many of their descendants, like my friend Ed, still occupy the land. Life is better now, thanks to modern conveniences, but it's still no bowl of cherries.

Some years ago, before the advent of cell phones, Ed and his wife, Ila, spent a long night in their car, waiting out a freak spring blizzard that piled snow in eight-foot drifts around their house. They'd been to town and as the weather worsened, hurried for home. They almost made it, too. They were stuck in their own ranch driveway, not more than a few hundred yards from their house, when the full fury of the storm hit. To risk a dash to the house in the whiteout would have been folly; many an old-time homesteader perished only yards from his doorstep, disoriented by a prairie blizzard. Ed and Ila stayed in the car until the next morning, when a neighbor came to their rescue on a snowmobile.

Tough birds, Ed and Ila. Tough birds, too, the sharp-tailed grouse. In winter they burrow into freshly fallen snow to escape the howling wind. In spring, the survivors gather on timeworn dancing grounds to celebrate the arrival of a new cycle of life on the plains. In summer, they take shelter from the heat by squatting on a breezy ridgetop or in the shade of chokecherry trees. But it is in autumn, when they wax fat on rosehips and frost-numbed grasshoppers, that the hunter knows them best.

I hunted sharptails for the first time in southwestern Saskatchewan almost forty years ago. I lived in Minnesota then, and some friends and I had made the thousand-mile trek to hunt geese in the wheat fields around the little town of Kindersley. We worked the huge flocks of snows, Canadas, and whitefronts that stage in this area in early fall, shooting from shallow pits chiseled at great cost of sweat and muscle from the prairie hardpan. In the mornings we hunted geese, in the afternoons we scouted geese, and at night we dug goose pits by lantern light. In the middle of the day, when we should have been resting, we hunted Hungarian partridge and sharp-tailed grouse. We were new to the country and wanted to see and experience as much as we could.

We looked for sharptails and Huns around abandoned home-steads, where trees and grass formed islands of cover in the expanses of wheat—or in the sandhills, where the soil and topography favored grazing over farming. As much as I liked the suspense of huddling in a clammy goose pit, scarcely daring to breathe while a flock of honking geese backpedaled down to our decoys, my fate was sealed when that first sharptail clattered up from a wild rose thicket. From then on, I wanted to hunt grouse.

The primary range of the plains sharptail—the subspecies that inhabits the northern plains—includes the eastern two-thirds of Montana, a slice of northeastern Wyoming, the western portions of Nebraska and North and South Dakota, and much of Alberta and Saskatchewan to the north. It is primarily a grassland bird, although it likes some brush or trees to round out its habitat. In Montana, the birds do best where shrub-filled coulees dissect the upland prairie, providing summer shade and refuge from winter storms.

Although the Conservation Reserve Program has been a godsend to sharptails and other plains wildlife since its inception in the 1980s, we are not likely to see a return to the days when thousands of grouse filled the air in a great roar of wings. Consider the reflections of Mrs. H. E. Crofford, a pioneer schoolteacher who traveled from Fargo, North Dakota, in 1871: "The grass that year was more than two feet high. . . . Chickens [sharptails] were thick. When we went out for a drive, as we sometimes did, the wheels of the vehicle or the horse's feet often crushed their eggs. I hated to see the wheel come up, dripping egg yolks. That wonderful grass waved like a sea in the sunlight, a forerunner of the wheat fields that would wave there in after years."

The homesteaders, who were more interested in meat than sport, began harvesting their birds about the middle of August. The young birds made easy targets and tender table fare. Today, most western states and provinces open the sharptail season in early September, when the birds are almost fully grown. This is the best time for hunting them because the birds are still in family groups and more inclined to hold for pointing dogs. Later in the fall they gather in large flocks and get progressively wilder and harder to approach.

Opening day usually finds me working a hay meadow adjacent to a brush-bordered stream shortly after sunrise. Last year I hadn't gone more than a quarter of a mile when my Brittany, Ollie, tightened up on a high-headed point. I walked in quickly and a dozen brown-and-white birds erupted from the bunchgrass, uttering the sharptail's familiar *cuk-cuk-cuk-cuk*. I knocked one down with my first shot but missed with the second. While I was reloading my over/under, three more birds flushed off to my left and followed the others over a rise and out of sight.

Mature sharptails sometimes fly more than a mile after being flushed, but early in the fall the birds often scatter and drop into cover within a few hundred yards. I followed their line of flight over the ridge to a draw blanketed with wild rose, snowberry, and choke-cherry. As I entered the cover, Ollie hesitated, took a few steps forward and froze on point. I got the single when it flushed and took two more birds over points farther down the coulee.

This was classic early season sharptail hunting. It doesn't always go so smoothly, even in September. But by late fall, when the cover has thinned and the birds have gathered into bigger flocks, conditions get tougher. Spooky birds, wild flushes, and long shots are typical after mid-October, although birds in Conservation Reserve grassland sometimes hold well for pointing dogs.

Because of the changing conditions, it's hard to generalize about guns and loads for sharptails. In September, I use a 12 or 20 gauge over/under choked improved cylinder and modified with No. 6 shot. Later in the fall, a full choke might work better on wild-flushing birds. For all-around use, modified choke is a good compromise.

Sharptail hunting is at its best early in the season when the young birds allow good dog work, the temperatures are ideal for camping, and the prairie scenery is at its autumn best. After a long day of hunting, a cold drink, and a good meal, a person can't be blamed for letting his imagination soar. I can look into the embers of my campfire and see a herd of bison bordered by a skulking pack of buffalo wolves, Lewis and Clark forging slowly up the Missouri, or perhaps a homesteader, an old hammer gun in one hand and brace of sharptails in the other, striding toward a humble log dwelling.

As the fire burns down and the last coals flicker and go out, the buffalo and wolves grow silent, Lewis and Clark vanish into the river mist, and the homesteader disappears into his cabin, which now stands empty, slowly returning to the prairie sod. Only the snow-bellied bird remains.

Chukars Aren't Easy

We used to rest on the west side of the Salmon River near Grangeville, Idaho, look across at the vertical slopes rising from the narrow fringe of sandy beach on the east side, and shudder at the prospect of hunting there. The slopes weren't really vertical, except for some solid spans of dark, rocky cliff. But they were steep enough to give that impression. Someone always mentioned the chukar hunter who fell from the cliffs and passed on to the great cheatgrass mountain in the sky.

I don't know how it affected the others, but I always watched my footing more closely when we started hunting again. I suspect that my partners, some of whom had been smokejumpers in their younger days, paid less attention to the topographical perils than I did. People who make their living jumping out of airplanes aren't squeamish about heights.

We eventually began hunting the slopes across the river—the friendlier portions of them. If we picked our route carefully, we could wind in and out of the canyons and above or below the precipices. It was satisfying in a masochistic way. Chukars were there, and that's the name of the game.

There are easier ways to hunt the red-legged birds. There's the jet boat routine, where you cruise the river until you spot birds, then go after them. It works well early in the season when the weather is hot and the birds are concentrated near water. Late-season snowstorms sometimes push chukars to lower elevations, making them more accessible to hunters. But most of my hunting has involved climbing the high, brown hills.

I've hunted chukars alone, but I don't like to. The country is steep and rugged. It's nice to have a partner or two in case of an emergency. I've never had a problem more serious than a leg cramp or a fall into a clump of prickly pear, but I breathe easier knowing someone will look for me if I have an accident.

Speaking of falling, the question is not whether you will, but how many times. There are two schools of thought: You can use your gun to break your fall and save your body, or you can use your body to break your fall and save your gun. One of my hunting partners has a once-pretty 20 gauge over/under with more tape holding it together than a running back's knees. The proponents of the second school have expensive taste in guns and a working man's salary. They also have a high pain threshold and believe human flesh will heal faster than fancy French walnut. I wear a leather shooting glove on my left hand, the hand I use to break my fall.

When it comes to equipment, all things pale in importance before a good pair of boots. Vibram (lug) soles are essential, and boots should fit well and be broken in. Just to be safe, I always carry moleskin in my hunting vest and use it at the first sign of a blister.

It had been several years since my last chukar trip when I got a call from my Missoula-based hunting partner, Joe Elliott. "I hear Idaho has lots of chukars this year," he said. "Why don't you drive over from Helena and stay at my house Wednesday night. If we get an early start we'll be hunting by noon the next day."

"Sounds great," I said. "Groucho has never pointed a chukar and I'm anxious to see what he can do."

As promised, the next day found us at the river looking up at the steep hillside we planned to hunt. We turned out our young Brittanys, Groucho and Rana, and headed up the slope. The climb was slow, hard work. We gauged our progress by keeping an eye on a lone ponderosa pine far above us. Whenever we stopped to catch our breath we noted with satisfaction the tree was inching closer, while our truck parked at the river was getting smaller. Steelhead anglers in the river below began to look like the little plastic fishermen you see on birthday cakes.

We followed a rocky gully for a time, then split up to look for chukar sign. I'd been climbing for about an hour when Groucho caught a whiff of scent and pointed upslope. I heard a clatter of wings in the rocks above me, and three chukars sailed past at the edge of shotgun range. I swung on the closest one and pulled the trigger. The bird tumbled down the slope and out of sight.

This was Groucho's first chukar and he had some things to learn about retrieving them. In steep terrain, downed chukars often roll and flutter a long way down the mountain. Good marking helps, but chukar dogs soon discover that birds often end up fifty yards or more below where they first hit the ground.

Groucho worked the scent downslope for ten or twenty yards, then returned to the place where the bird had fallen. His eyes had told him where the bird should be and he was having a hard time believing his nose. Finally I went down the hill with him until he sorted out the trail. At the end of it lay a dead chukar.

I love all the western game birds, but there is something special about chukars. The birds' blood-red beak and red legs contrast sharply with their olive-gray back and breast. Black and chestnut vertical stripes on their sides give them the look of feathered zebras. A mature chukar tips the scales at a little over a pound—bigger than a Hungarian partridge but slightly smaller than a ruffed grouse.

Brought here from India, Pakistan, and Afghanistan in the 1930s, chukars prospered on the dry, rocky slopes above western rivers like the Salmon, Snake, Malheur, Owyhee, and Columbia. Their success is strongly linked to cheatgrass, an annual grass introduced to North America from the Mediterranean region. Because it sprouts in the fall and provides green shoots throughout much of the winter, cheatgrass provides a dependable food supply when other foods are scarce.

After resting a few minutes I put the bird in my vest and began picking my way through the sagebrush and slide rock. I could hear a dog bell upslope so I knew Joe and Rana were up there somewhere. While I studied the terrain above me, I heard Joe shoot; a few seconds later a dozen birds rocketed down the hill toward me. Chukars passing overhead don't leave much time for analysis. I barely had time to mount the gun, catch up with a bird, and slap the trigger. I tagged one with the improved cylinder barrel of my over/under but the rest of the birds were gone before I could get off a second shot. The bird's momentum carried it far down the mountain where it hit and somersaulted down the slope.

This time Groucho made the long trek downslope without a hitch. He had just delivered the bird to me when three more chukars lifted from a grassy knob above. These were farther out, speeding downhill and crossing. I missed with the first barrel but scored with the second. Groucho plunged back down the mountain to retrieve it.

I felt a little smug after connecting on three of my first four shots, but chukars have a way of evening the score. The trouble started when my feet slipped in the loose rocks as I moved in to flush a bird Groucho had pointed in a rockslide below me. I didn't get off a shot. Then I missed a downhill screamer that flushed below me. A few minutes later I missed the safety catch on what would have been the easiest shot of the day. I got a fourth bird eventually, but not before I had blown several more chances.

Although nothing can prepare hunters for the kind of shots they may get while sweating their way across a chukar slope, a trip to a sporting clays course will help, especially if it has some changes in elevation. But sporting clays can't simulate the bad footing, fatigue, and rubbery knees that afflict chukar hunters. Most shots are taken downslope, which requires getting the muzzle ahead of and *below* the target—it's not a shot wingshooters have much chance to practice.

I've found I can sometimes tip the odds in my favor if I'm able to work my way below the birds before they flush. Air wafting upslope on a warm afternoon will carry chukar scent to a pointing dog and, if the cover is good, birds below him will hold well. When my dog points downhill, I try looping below him; if I succeed without disturbing the covey, I know they'll have to come out over me or pass in front of me, because chukars rarely fly uphill. Both of these shots are easier than trying to hit a bird that's screaming straight downhill.

Once I've moved a covey, I mark its line of flight. Chukars always fly downhill, but after the initial dive they often turn and follow the contour. I drop downslope a bit, then follow them as quickly as I can. If the covey scatters, and I can get there before they regroup, I often have excellent singles shooting. That's when a dog is a tremendous asset, since the singles tend to sit tight.

Pointers get the nod over flushing breeds with most chukar hunters for the simple reason that it is difficult to move quickly on a chukar hill. Chukars like to run and don't always hold for point, but some do. Pointed birds, obviously, give hunters more time to maneuver into position for a shot.

Any dog is useful when it comes to retrieving downed birds. The late Ted Trueblood, who knew chukar hunting as well as anyone, summed it up this way: "No matter how carefully you mark them down, no man can find a chukar that lands running in thick sagebrush or plunges down into a hole among the rocks, as they often will do." My hunting partner once winged a chukar that we couldn't find; after several minutes of looking, his Brittany pointed into a pile of rocks. We took the rock pile apart piece by piece and found the bird.

Chukar country is hard on dogs as well as hunters. I carry two quart bottles of water and sometimes it's not enough. Dogs whose feet haven't been toughened by plenty of fieldwork will develop sore pads. Dog boots have saved the day on more than one of my chukar hunting trips.

Theories on guns and loads for chukar hunting abound. I hunt with an over/under, but the two-shot limitation has cost me plenty of chukars. A sleeper boiling out after the covey rise is not unusual, and I wish I had a dollar for every time I've been caught with an empty gun. I like improved cylinder and modified chokes with No. 6 shot. Although I hunt with a 12 gauge, there's no question a lighter gauge will leave you fresher at the end of the day.

Speaking of the end of the day, my knees tell me when it's time to start back down the mountain. By 2 p.m. on the day of my chukar hunt with Joe, my knees had long since quit whispering and had begun to shout. Far below at the river I could see Joe and Rana walking along the road toward the truck. We'd tried to keep in contact, but sometimes it's hard to do in steep terrain. Later he explained that he'd hit a bird that locked its wings and sailed halfway to the river. He'd dropped down to look for it and didn't have the energy to climb all the way back up again.

By the time I got to the road my feet felt like they'd been through a paper shredder. For hunters whose knees have suffered years of abuse, going downhill at the end of the day is harder than going up in the morning. At the truck, Joe and I compared notes. He had fanned on a couple of covey rises, slipped and fell several times, and managed to scratch down only one chukar.

"I should have had at least four," he said.

"Don't feel bad," I replied. "I should have had my limit with all the chances I had."

Sitting by the river cleaning our birds we could hear the taunting *chuk-chuk-chuk-chuk* calls of birds high on the mountain. I'm not sure of the exact translation, but it didn't sound polite. On the plus side, we'd gotten off the hill in one piece, with only our egos bruised. There is a saying among hunters addicted to pursuing chukars: You hunt them the first time for sport, but after that it's for revenge.

Sonoran Safari

———✦———

The Arizona desert can be a daunting place when the wind blows. Joe Elliott and I had driven south from Montana in January for a week of Gambel's quail hunting, and had set up camp on public land about thirty miles north of the small town of Wickenburg. As we sat around the campfire that night under a clear, calm sky, a windstorm was the last thing on our minds.

About 2 a.m. the sound of tent canvas flapping wildly in the wind awakened us. A cooking pot whizzed off into the desert, and a moment later our camp stove and stove stand went down with a crash. We bolted from our cots and grabbed boots and flashlights. The tent, an old Coleman cabin-style model that had seen heroic duty over the years, was listing and close to collapse.

We quickly rounded up extra ropes and staked out guy lines from the tent's corner poles. Then we stumbled around the desert gathering up plates, pans and other items we had left sitting out. A few things disappeared forever; they probably came to earth in the next county.

By morning the wind had subsided. The whole episode seemed like a bad dream. "I wonder how hard it blew last night," Joe said, his cold fingers wrapped around a steaming mug of coffee. His eyes were red and his voice scratchy, like he'd swallowed a tablespoon of sand.

"If we were closer to the ocean I'd say it was a hurricane," I replied, spitting out grit. "There's sand in everything, including my teeth."

There was nothing left to do but gather our strength and go looking for quail. We unloaded our Brittanys, Groucho and Rana, and headed for a sandy wash where we had noticed quail tracks the night before. We hadn't gone far down the mesquite-lined draw when Groucho's bell stopped, started, then stopped again. I caught a glimpse of a Gambel's quail darting ahead, its jaunty black topknot bobbing through the green prickly pear.

"There's a covey ahead!" I yelled. A quail flushed, then a bunch of quail took off in a rush of wings. I couldn't see exactly where they put down, but I had a rough idea. After a fifteen-minute search we bumped a single, then a pair of birds. Joe scratched down the single with his second barrel, and I tumbled a cockbird from the pair. We spent the next hour chasing this covey, then stumbled into another one on the way back to camp. By the time we arrived there, we had eight quail between us.

Although Gambel's quail look gray from a distance, in hand they are striking birds, especially the males with their black face rimmed in white, chestnut crown, and cream-colored belly splotched with black. Females lack the distinctive head markings but like the males they have a dark topknot and rusty flanks streaked with white.

In camp we ate lunch, watered the dogs, cleaned birds, and enjoyed the shirtsleeve warmth. When the temperature began to drop later in the afternoon we drove to another streambed that had an intermittent flow of water. Mesquite and paloverde trees bordered the sandy wash, while saguaro cactus, ocotillo, prickly pear, and yucca dotted the adjacent hillsides. We found the first covey not far from the truck; they flushed out of range and we followed them a few hundred yards up the wash where we rousted them again. This time they scattered into the desert.

Working back and forth through the area several times produced a number of points and close flushes. Gambel's quail are strong runners, but once a covey breaks up the singles hold well. They don't give off much scent in the dry climate and it's easy for dogs to miss them. The best strategy is to cover the area thoroughly, starting and stopping frequently. Sometimes if you hang around long enough the birds will begin to move and put out more scent for the dogs.

I shoot a 12 gauge over/under choked improved cylinder and modified, but a 20 gauge will do the job. Shot size is more important than gauge. I like standard trap loads with No. 7½ shot (1⅛ oz.). Some hunters drop down to No. 6 if birds are flushing wild. No. 8 shot is too light. Gambel's quail are tough birds and if they aren't well hit they'll take off running and disappear into the desert, usually into a packrat midden. My dogs have dug them out of such places several times, a process that makes me nervous because snakes also use these burrows. I've yet to run into a rattlesnake, but all my Arizona hunts have been in December and January when nighttime temperatures drop close to freezing.

Our afternoon hunt yielded three more quail apiece. Groucho had a couple of encounters with cactus that required my help. The area we were hunting had a scattering of jumping cholla, a cactus that sheds small, spiny segments onto the ground where unsuspecting dogs can step on them. When Groucho stopped and began biting at his paw, I guessed correctly he had a piece of cholla in his foot. I either wear leather gloves or carry them in my hunting vest, along with a comb and needle-nose pliers. Dislodging pieces of cactus from a dog's foot or face with a comb will save your fingers from getting stabbed. Leather gloves help but spines can go through them. Pliers come in handy when spines become embedded in a paw or leg. Dogs have mishaps with prickly pear, too, but cholla is the main villain. It's best to avoid areas heavily infested with it.

Due to the rugged nature of the Sonoran desert, most dogs visiting for the first time end up with sore feet. I keep a close eye on my dogs and use Lewis dog boots at the first sign of distress. But dogs aren't the only ones to have cactus problems. Almost everything growing in the desert has thorns or spines and hunters get punctured from time to time. Large thorns can be pulled out easily but small spines may require a tweezers. I carry a good pair that will grasp and hold a small spine or sliver. Once while hunting I tripped and brushed against a waist-high prickly pear cactus. I had at least a hundred spines in my arm, most of them tiny hairlike ones that I could hardly see. It took me more than an hour to get them out. I thought I'd be sore for days, but by the next morning my arm felt fine.

The sun sets quickly in the desert. One minute it's warm and sunny, the next minute it's dark and getting cold. One night at sundown we began a firewood search, grabbing whatever dead branches, sticks, and chunks of wood we could find. We got a blaze going in the fire ring and sat down to enjoy dinner and a cold brew. Exhausted from travel and hunting, we sat half asleep in our folding chairs when the campfire hissed and exploded, sending a shower of sparks skyward. I jumped up to brush the sparks off my coat, and Joe did an Irish jig of his own. Groucho, who had been snoozing next to the fire, hid under the truck.

We sat down again but it wasn't long before another explosion sent us scrambling. Fortunately there was no wind to carry off the embers so we didn't set the desert on fire. Many desert trees and shrubs have a high oil content but not all of them explode. Mesquite burns slow and hot, forming a beautiful bed of coals. Our mystery wood kept us hopping until we finally gave up and doused the fire.

The next morning we explored an arroyo a few miles from camp and put up a small covey of quail after a half-hour walk. We scattered the birds and bagged a few singles as dark clouds rolled in from the west. We missed more than we hit, which we blamed on the darkening sky. Gambel's quail make challenging targets even in bright sunshine, but on cloudy days the birds' grayish backs and tails make them especially hard to see against the muted desert landscape. Some hunters swear by shooting glasses with yellow lenses that add sharpness and contrast.

There were a few sprinkles on the truck windshield by the time we got back to camp. The radio confirmed we were in for a change in weather—a front was moving in from California and the twenty-four-hour forecast promised colder temperatures and rain. After lunch the rain began to beat a steady tattoo on the tent roof. Joe tempted fate when he asked, "It's the desert, right? How much can it rain in the desert?"

By the next day the Sonoran desert had answered: It can rain a lot. By the time the storm subsided we had named the tent "Old Leaky." To help pass the time I thumbed through my Audubon guide to North American deserts. "It says here the Sonoran is considered moist by desert standards."

Joe shot me a disgusted look. "No kidding."

"It also says prolonged winter rains can drive hibernating snakes out of the ground and up into trees. We could have rattlesnakes, of which there are eleven species in Arizona, hanging from the branches like Christmas ornaments."

The rain stopped during the night and the next day dawned clear and cold. We spent the morning drying our gear and waiting for the roads to drain a bit before setting out again. That afternoon we tried a new spot a few miles from camp where the desert climbed toward rugged brown foothills. Rana and Groucho ranged in front of us, threading their way among prickly pear and thorn bushes.

As we worked along a ridge we heard quail calling ahead. A short time later both dogs' bells fell silent. Gambel's quail don't wait around for dogs and hunters, so Joe and I jogged ahead. I spotted Groucho on point just as a covey roared off behind a mesquite tree. Even a small covey makes a racket when it flushes, but judging by the noise this one had to be a "winter covey" containing dozens of birds.

Gambel's quail numbers fluctuate from year to year, mostly in response to winter precipitation. Briefly put, winter rains produce abundant green plants, setting the stage for a good hatch the following spring. Quail grow fat on the vitamin-rich plants and go into breeding season in peak condition. Green plants also promote higher insect populations, which are vital to survival of newly hatched quail. Gambel's chicks depend on beetles, worms, caterpillars, and grasshoppers the first few days of their lives. In dry years, when plant life and insects are scarce, desert quail may fail to mate.

Joe and I were now reaping the benefits of several wet winters in succession. As we sweated our way up the steep, rock-strewn hillside in the direction the covey had flown, Groucho and Rana rewarded us with several points. This area had better grass cover than we had found down lower, providing lots of hiding spots for quail. I connected on two singles in a row, then missed a couple. Joe made a good shot on a bird that barreled downhill like a miniature chukar. Several quail flushed and darted behind trees or bushes and escaped. As we circled the area we flushed and bagged several more birds.

Groucho is gone now, but I think he liked hunting Gambel's quail more than he did any other bird despite the inhospitable terrain. For him, I'm sure it was the intoxicating scent. I like hunting them too, but it goes deeper. I fell in love with the Sonoran desert with its candelabra-shaped saguaros and abundant wildlife on my first visit. I've returned many times, in good quail years and bad, and enjoyed every trip. Trekking through the desert on a Sonoran safari, when states farther north are locked in the deep freeze, is a great way to finish the hunting season.

Edgar's Bird

———— ·❧· ————

Remember that old Simon and Garfunkel tune, "The Sound of Silence"? If you're using your ears to follow a Brittany's bell through manzanita brush and live oaks along the Mexican border, silence is a wonderful sound. It means you may be closing in on a covey of Mearns quail.

I scrambled up the rocky slope and found Chief crouched beneath the branches of an evergreen oak, his eyes locked on a sun-dappled patch of ground where something had scratched up the dead leaves and forest litter. I took a deep breath, readied my 20 gauge over/under, and moved ahead of the dog. Nothing. The next step detonated an explosion of Mearns quail so close I could nearly have touched them with my shotgun. The first shot with the skeet choke sent a shower of twigs and leaves cascading to the ground. When the last bird in the covey flashed through an opening I snapped off another shot. This time, along with more leaves, a few feathers circled to earth.

Chief' s bell tinkled busily for ten seconds and then stopped . . . a good sign. His bell started up again and when he emerged from the shadows, walking slowly, he held a cock quail in his mouth. It had white polka dots on its sides, a chestnut breast, and a black belly and rump. Its face—striped with bluish-black and white—reminded me of a painted-up college kid at a football game.

Named for Edgar Alexander Mearns, a naturalist and U.S. Army surgeon who led a biological survey of the Southwestern border region in the late 1800s, the little clown-faced birds are also known as harlequin quail, Montezuma quail, and, in the early days, Massena quail. In Mexico, where they're more abundant, they are sometimes called *codorniz pinta*, painted quail.

Joe Elliott called to me from across the canyon: "Get one?"

"Sure did," I yelled back. "Edgar's bird."

Our quail-hunting trip to southern Arizona had its origins several years earlier on East Africa's Mount Kenya. Joe had just finished a teaching stint at the University of Nairobi and I had joined him for a month of travel through Kenya's game parks. Reading about Mount Kenya, I learned that Dr. Mearns had accompanied Teddy Roosevelt to Africa in 1908, serving as the expedition's naturalist. Roosevelt hailed him as "the best field naturalist and collector in the United States, and a superb shot." During that trip Mearns and a companion climbed Mount Kenya, where they collected "1,112 birds, of 210 species . . . 1,320 mammals and 771 reptiles."

Joe and I and another friend spent several days on Mount Kenya, scrambling to the top of Point Lenana at more than 16,000 feet and gazing in awe at the strange plants and animals, some of which exist nowhere else in the world. We had all we could do to get up and down the mountain without oxygen, let alone collect thousands of plant and animal specimens. A tough man, that Dr. Mearns. Now, a decade after following his footsteps up Mount Kenya, we were retracing his tracks along the Mexican border, searching for the quail named in his honor.

Just getting to southern Arizona had been an adventure. We had driven south from Montana in January in my old Ford van, which I had adapted for traveling with bird dogs. The back of the van had room for four travel crates on the floor—two for Joe's springer spaniels and two for my Brittany pup and a black Lab. A fifth dog, my male Brittany, Chief, rode on the floor behind my seat.

The van's only drawback was its poor traction on snow and ice, both of which had vexed us in the 1,400 miles between Montana and southern Arizona. By the time we dropped off the Mogollon Rim south of Flagstaff, the snow had turned to rain. Unlike summer rains, which arrive in the form of afternoon thunderstorms, winter rains in Arizona arise from major frontal systems that sweep in from the coast. These storms, accompanied by strong winds and steady rain, often last a day or two.

We camped for the night in the desert south of Sedona, and in the morning we stopped at Fort Verde State Historical Park, where Dr. Mearns had been stationed in the 1880s. At Fort Verde we toured the surgeon's quarters and other buildings, and I picked up a copy of a booklet called "Birds in Arizona's Sedona–Oak Creek Area, Observed and Taken as Specimens by Dr. Edgar Mearns, January, 1885." In this book Mearns describes his first encounter with the quail eventually named in his honor:

I noticed that the sexes were plainly distinguishable when flying, even at a distance. They ran and flew a short distance alternately until well up on the steep hillside of sliding rocks that were covered with long grass and low scrub oaks, affording the very finest kind of cover. As I clambered up this difficult slope, one after another they flew up before me, always from right in front of me, uttering their singular notes, and generally taking me when I was badly balanced and unprepared. I got three shots and brought down two birds, a pair.

That afternoon we drove south through on-and-off showers and spent the night about fifty miles south of Tucson in the little town of Patagonia. Early the next morning while walking down the main street I saw a truck with Michigan plates and a couple of English setters in the back. I figured the setters belonged to the two hunters I could see through the window of the nearby café, so I went in to chat. One of the men turned out to be part-time Montanan Jim Harrison, author of *Legends of the Fall* and other literary works. Between bites of their huevos rancheros, Harrison and his partner graciously gave me a rundown on where to look for Mearns quail.

After stocking up on groceries, Joe and I headed east on a gravel road that winds through the Coronado National Forest toward the San Rafael Valley. The rain had stopped during the night, but ragged gray clouds rested atop the peaks of the Patagonia Mountains.

We hadn't gone far into the snow-powdered hills before we ran into trouble. The road crosses Harshaw Creek in numerous places and at the first crossing, the creek, normally just a trickle, was now a muddy torrent from the heavy rains. Several vehicles sat lined up on both sides of the crossing, their drivers standing outside watching a backhoe operator rearrange the creekbed.

After a half-hour of filling and leveling, the backhoe jockey parked his machine on the far side of the wash, jumped down and sent the first truck across from the other side. "I'm glad we're not first," Joe said.

The vehicle, a small pickup, made it across okay, its driver looking relieved as the truck sloshed out of the creek and past us. When our turn came, we too made the crossing without incident. The backhoe operator, a Hispanic man in his thirties, had left his backhoe and was now hoofing it up the road, so we offered him a ride.

"Where are you headed?" Joe asked.

"Harshaw. About a mile up the road," he replied.

"Jump in. Grab a seat on the cooler and we'll give you a lift."

"Thanks," he said. "Does your dog bite?"

"Only quail," I said, laughing.

"A quail dog! What's his name?"

"Chief."

"*El jefe de las codornices*," he said, scratching Chief's ear. "Boss of the quail."

We let our rider out at the old mining town of Harshaw and continued south toward the Mexican border. The sun peeked out from behind the clouds and quickly melted the remaining snow. The countryside looked like anything but the Arizona desert. We were in the mountains, climbing to an elevation of about 5,000 feet, and instead of saguaros and paloverdes we were surrounded by evergreen oaks, junipers, and manzanita. Here and there a leafless sycamore with spreading gray branches shaded the creek. Lush grasses—grama, beardgrass, and bluestem—stood knee-high under the oak trees. Ideal Mearns quail habitat, according to Jim Harrison.

We pulled off the road at a likely spot and uncased our shotguns. Since we intended this to be a hasty recon to stretch our legs and get a feel for the country, we took only one dog, Chief. We hadn't gone far up the steep canyon when the little drama I described at the beginning of this chapter unfolded.

While I waited for Joe to join me on my side of the wash, I poured Chief a drink in the collapsible bowl I carry in my game vest. The day was warming despite the cool breeze rustling through the leaves of the oak trees. When Joe arrived we spent a few minutes admiring the first Mearns quail either of us had seen up close.

"Check out those claws," Joe said, pointing to the bird's half-inch long, scythe-shaped toenails. "That's what they use to scratch for breakfast."

Mearns quail prefer digging for the bulbs of wood sorrel and the tubers of sedges, but they also eat acorns, seeds, and insects.

After Chief had rested and drunk his fill, we walked in the direction the covey had gone. Mearns quail don't fly far, and they are notorious for sitting tight after being scattered. A short time later Chief's bell stopped again.

"I think he's got one," Joe said.

I was screened out by the trees and before I could work my way into shooting position a single whirred out. Joe had a clear shot and grassed it just before it could escape behind an alligator juniper.

Chief brought it to me and I held it next to my bird for comparison. A cinnamon-colored hen with brown and black markings, it had an almost pinkish tinge.

We crisscrossed the area a couple of times and Chief pointed two more quail, one of which went into my game vest. The remaining birds in the covey had found secure hiding places and weren't about to move, so we headed back to the van for a cold drink and a sandwich.

After lunch we drove down the road until we found a track branching off into the national forest. The road wound down and across a sandy wash and continued on into a series of oak-covered hills dissected by steep, dark canyons. The sun-cured grama and bluestem appeared only lightly grazed and it looked like good quail country. We found a flat spot for the tent and set up camp. Then we grabbed our shotguns and headed into the hills with Chief and the springers, Zeke and Zelda. We split up so the springers wouldn't bust in on Chief's points—should there be any—and agreed to meet back at camp in a few hours.

Just above a stock pond on a grassy hillside, Chief tiptoed to a point. This time I was ready for the noisy flush of Edgar's birds, and I dropped one with my first shot. Over the next twenty minutes I bagged a couple of singles, then moved on toward the top of a long ridge dotted with Mexican oaks. When I glimpsed a Coues whitetail slipping through the trees ahead of me, I thought of a Mearns quail hunt described by Jack O'Connor in his book *Game in the Desert*, published in 1939:

> I had hunted a half-hour and got five or six birds when I kicked one up that had hidden under the leaves of a yucca. He flew straight away, and when he was directly over a patch of chaparral I let him have it. He crumpled in mid-air and dropped straight into the brush. The moment he hit, a white-tail buck jumped out of that little brush patch. Despite my astonishment I automatically gave him the full-choke barrel. At twenty yards the charge penetrated to his heart and I came down the mountain that day with the rarest deer and a mess of the rarest game birds in the United States. Such is luck!

During the next two hours Chief nailed three more coveys; I shot up a pocketful of shells, collecting several more quail. I could hear the bark of Joe's shotgun a couple of draws over so I knew he and the springers were having similar luck.

Back at camp we counted our quail. We had a total of twelve, not bad for two gringos from the far north. Sitting around the campfire that night after a grilled quail dinner, Joe hoisted a cold Corona in Chief's honor: "*El jefe de las codornices*, I salute you." Then we toasted Zeke and Zelda, the quail, and our hero, Dr. Edgar Mearns, the indefatigable naturalist who had inspired our journey.

Jailhouse Blues

———◆◆◆———

We got up before dawn to let the dogs out of their travel crates and greet the new day—the first morning of a long-awaited January quail hunt in southeastern Arizona. Steve McMorran and I had left the cold and snow of Montana three days earlier; now, 1,400 miles from home, we were camped in the Sulphur Springs Valley near Willcox. We had stopped in southern Utah to pick up Steve's twenty-year-old daughter, Jamie, who wasn't planning on bird hunting but wanted to poke around the desert with us.

We weren't exactly camped in a wilderness, but Willcox was thirty miles away and we didn't expect to see anyone but possibly another hunter or two or a cowboy out checking his cattle. We had passed some houses in a small settlement on the main road several miles away, which we assumed were occupied by ranch hands or employees of the nearby state prison at Fort Grant.

Standing in the darkness waiting for the dogs to stretch their legs, I saw off in the distance headlights moving in our direction. Quail hunters getting an early start to avoid the mid-day heat? Javelina hunters? I was surprised to see other hunters on the move so early in this out-of-the-way place. Surprise turned to disappointment when I saw a second set of headlights, then a third and a fourth. "Steve, I can't believe it," I said. "We just drove 1,400 miles to get to the middle of the Chihuahuan desert and the place is crawling with hunters."

"I guess we'd better roust Jamie and go hunting while there's still a few quail left," he replied.

Despite daytime temperatures that often reach seventy degrees in mid-winter, the Arizona desert gets cold at night. Where we were camped, at an elevation of 4,000 feet, it usually freezes. Mornings are chilly until the sun has been up for an hour or so.

By the time we brewed coffee, the sun was peeking over the Pinaleno Mountains to the east. I had hunted the area before, so I suggested we drive a mile down the road to an area where I had found scaled quail in previous years. Scalies get their name from the black markings on their breast and belly that form a scalloped pattern. Often called blue quail or cottontops, these sleek birds have a bluish-gray appearance when they're hot-footing across the desert or in flight. They lack the comma-shaped topknot of the Gambel's quail, Arizona's most common species. Instead they have a bushy, white-tipped crest, hence the nickname "cottontop."

Just as we pulled off the dusty track near a stock tank, an official-looking truck roared up behind us. Two men with guns and badges jumped out. "Jeez," said Jamie, "these Arizona game wardens sure are aggressive." But a quick look at the truck dispelled the notion we were in for a license check. Instead of Arizona Game and Fish Department, it said Arizona Department of Corrections.

After an inspection of our truck satisfied them we weren't harboring fugitives, the older of the two, a dead ringer for Wilfred Brimley, explained the situation. "We've got two convicts out here," he growled. "They cut a hole in the fence at Fort Grant last night shortly after dark and they've been on the run ever since. We've been trailing 'em with bloodhounds all night."

"You mean these guys have been loose out here while we've been asleep in our tent?" I asked.

Wilfred spat a stream of tobacco juice and wiped his white walrus mustache with the sleeve of his coat. "'Fraid so."

"Do you want us to pack up and leave?"

"No, that won't be necessary just yet. But you need to go back to your camp and lock up any food, water, clothing, or weapons—we don't want them to get ahold of anything that'll help 'em escape."

The radio crackled in the truck and Wilfred barked, "Get that, Sam."

His sidekick, a young guy who looked more like a college student than a prison guard, hustled back to the cab. When he emerged he pointed toward brown hills several miles distant. "See the canyon that comes down beneath that big gray rock outcrop? That's where the dogs are now. They're headed this way."

Jamie's eyes widened. She asked the question that was on all our minds. "So are these guys killers or bank robbers, or what?"

"No, they're in for drug trafficking—but we consider them dangerous," said Wilfred.

"Is it okay if we keep hunting?" asked Steve.

"Yes, once you get your food and gear secured. But keep your eyes open and be sure to keep your truck locked. You'll see us around. We have several vehicles in this area. We'll catch 'em—it's just a matter of time."

With that, they jumped in their truck and took off, leaving us looking at each other in disbelief. On the way back to camp we discussed our options. Pack up and leave? Keep hunting? Sit in camp with loaded shotguns? Finally we decided to hunt until noon, then re-evaluate. We'd be hunting in open country where it would be hard for anyone to sneak up on us, let alone convicts clad in orange jumpsuits. But we were certain of one thing: if they weren't caught we'd break camp before nightfall.

Once we'd stowed our food and water in the truck and returned to our hunting spot, I let my Brittany, Groucho, out of his travel crate. I knew he'd point quail, but I wondered aloud if he'd point jailbirds. We laughed nervously, hoping we wouldn't find out.

Steve had never hunted quail so I explained the drill. "Keep an eye on Groucho—if he points, or if he's out of sight and his bell stops, we have to get there in a hurry. These scalies are runners and they'll be moving ahead. If you see them, rush in and try to get them to fly. Once we break up a covey the singles will hold tight. That's when we'll get our best shooting."

Typical Arizona scaled quail habitat lay before us: open grassland interspersed with occasional prickly pear cactus, soapweed yucca, "wait-a-minute" thorn, and scattered shrubs and mesquite trees. We had walked only about a quarter of a mile when Groucho veered sharply to the left, pointed, then resumed a stealthy walk. I motioned to Steve and Jamie to follow him. The start-and-stop routine continued for seventy yards—then the covey flushed at the edge of shotgun range. We marked them down and had just started to move ahead when a lone quail buzzed up in front of Steve and Jamie. Startled, Jamie jumped two feet in the air. Laughing at Jamie, Steve hadn't fired a shot.

Jamie smiled sheepishly. "Dang, that thing scared me. That was a quail, right?"

"Naw, that was one of those jailbirds they're looking for," Steve kidded. "How am I supposed to shoot a quail if you're jumping over the moon every time one takes off?"

In truth we were all a little keyed up. Jamie's reaction broke the tension and gave us a good laugh.

"Let's get after the covey," I said. "If Groucho points a bird or if we kick one up, there should be more in the area. We'll want to work back and forth several times."

We hadn't gone 300 yards when Groucho wheeled and pointed. This time Jamie hung back while Steve moved in, shotgun ready. A quail skittered out of the bunchgrass and Steve bagged his first blue quail. I took a step and two birds flushed off to my left; I dropped one with the improved cylinder barrel of my Browning 12 gauge and missed the other.

Groucho was occupied with Steve's quail, so I hurried to the spot where I had seen mine fall. Blue quail are notorious escape artists; if they aren't hit hard they'll streak away into the desert. This one, though, was dead and lying in plain sight. Groucho delivered Steve's bird to me, nuzzled the one already in my hand, and bolted away to chase down more of the alluring scent.

We circled the area a few times and flushed several more singles. Steve collected one and missed another, while I got one and missed two more. I always marvel at how fast a blue quail can make its getaway. Coming from Montana where my late-season hunting consists of pheasants and mallards I'm not ready for a seven-ounce quail that seems jet-propelled. I know it's an illusion—quail and pheasants top out at about the same speed and a mallard in full flight will put both in the shade—but their small size and explosive flush make blue quail tricky targets. Once I've had a few days to adjust, my shooting gets better.

After walking another hour we crossed a sandy wash; Groucho came to a sudden halt on the far side. As we hurried ahead a small covey lifted in good gun range. We each shot twice and brought down a bird apiece. During the next twenty minutes we located a few singles but the rest of the covey melted away into the desert.

By now the morning had begun to heat up. Despite several drinks from our water bottles, Groucho was hot and panting hard. It was time to get back to the truck and find a stock tank where he could take a swim.

Driving back to camp we ran into the prison guards again. Wilfred gave us a progress report. "The convicts are out of the canyon and headed south along the base of the hills," he said, pointing to the low line of hills a scant half-mile from our camp. "We've got a couple dozen men in the brush out there waiting for them."

Back at camp we laid our quail in the shade and opened cold drinks. We kept our guns loaded. I let my black Lab, Jenny, out of the truck to stand guard, despite her propensity for licking strangers' faces. At least she has a loud bark, I reasoned. Steve made sandwiches while Jamie stood on the truck tailgate with binoculars and gave us a blow-by-blow account of the action.

"I can see three guys—no, four guys—in camouflage getting out of a truck. They've got guns. Now they're walking into the desert."

We all had a turn with binoculars, and sure enough, we could see several vehicles deployed at strategic points along the range of hills. This was getting interesting. I half expected to hear bloodhounds baying in the distance.

A half hour passed, then an hour. We started to wonder if Wilfred's confidence about catching the convicts had been more for our benefit than a realistic assessment. Then Jamie announced, "I see a bunch of guys walking back toward the truck. Hey, they're all coming out!"

"That means one of two things," I said. "Either they've got the convicts or they're giving up. We'll find out soon enough."

Before long our friends from the prison stopped by to give us the news—they had captured the escapees. I felt like hugging Wilfred, but I shook his hand instead. It would be a major understatement to say we felt relieved. We didn't want to break camp and leave all those blue quail behind.

That night, to celebrate, we marinated our quail in Italian dressing and grilled them over mesquite coals. Accompanied by fried potatoes and onions, salad and a good bottle of wine, they were the perfect antidote for the jailhouse blues.

Hunting the Sagebrush Sasquatch

"Try to shoot a young one," I said. "They're the best eating." Thus I advised my hunting partner, Joe Elliott, as we stood watching the sun creep over the horizon and paint the eastern Montana prairie in shades of gold. We'd driven from our homes in western Montana last September to hunt North America's largest grouse. After spending the night camped near the small town of Malta, we got an early start and drove south toward a public tract where we'd found sage grouse in previous years. This is cowboy country, just north of the Missouri River and the sprawling C.M. Russell National Wildlife Refuge.

There are still plenty of cowboys and sage grouse in Montana, but times are changing. The open range is largely a thing of the past, and these days some cowboys round up their cattle with four-wheelers and motorbikes. Sage grouse, too, have been losing a gradual war of attrition across the West. The big birds need sagebrush, and sagebrush has too often been poisoned, burned, and plowed to make room for grassland, farms, and condos.

While Joe and his Brittany, Gret, made a swing toward an old corral off in the distance, I walked through knee-high sagebrush toward a small reservoir a half-mile away. Along the way my Brittany, Ollie, disappeared over a rise, and when his bell grew silent, I hurried to the brow of the hill. As I approached the point where I'd last heard the bell, a large brown bird rose from the sage, too far for a shot. Then another, closer bird cleared the sage and peeled away. I swung my 12 gauge over/under ahead of his beak, pulled the trigger, and watched him fold.

Ollie soon had the big male grouse in tow—so much for shooting a small, tender one. Ollie managed to haul him most of the way to me before spitting him out. Considering the warm morning, the loose feathers in his mouth, and the size of the bird, I didn't blame him. I would have spit him out, too. I'd shot the Sasquatch of the grouse world—a mature male sage grouse weighing upwards of five pounds.

Sage grouse often receive bad press when it comes to edibility, but they make excellent table fare early in the year when their diet consists of green plants and insects. Young birds are tender and good, especially when cut into pieces, marinated, and grilled over coals. Big bombers, like the one I shot, are best tenderized in a slow cooker and used to make stew.

Later in the fall, when the birds shift to a sagebrush diet (they're called sage grouse for a reason), the meat gets darker and stronger. Sage grouse need to be field-dressed promptly and iced down as soon as possible. A bird that spends hours stewing in its own juices in the back of your game vest on a warm day won't win any culinary prizes.

While there's no question the sage hen is our largest grouse, hunters and outdoor writers tend to exaggerate. Sage grouse the size of turkeys don't exist. Biologist Robert Patterson, who wrote *The Sage Grouse in Wyoming*, weighed hundreds of them in the course of his research. He found that mature males weigh five to seven pounds in winter and spring, but less during hunting season. A five-pound sage grouse in September, when most are taken by hunters, is a big one. Females average three pounds or so in winter but weigh less than three pounds in early fall. Of course, there are exceptions: In a Montana study of breeding grouse, one Boone & Crockett male tipped the scales at nearly nine pounds.

Like the bison they once co-existed with on the western plains, sage grouse need wide-open spaces to survive. When human presence increases, the birds decline. The latest threat is energy development, especially coal bed methane. When noise from generators, truck traffic, and compressors reverberates across the prairie, grouse are driven from ancestral strutting grounds. Adding to their woes, sage grouse are vulnerable to the recently introduced West Nile virus, a mosquito-borne illness that affects horses and wild birds as well as humans.

While greater sage grouse continue to have strongholds in Montana, Wyoming, Idaho, Nevada, and Oregon, they have declined or even disappeared in many parts of the West. Between 1965 and 1985, sage grouse numbers dropped an estimated 50 percent throughout the region. The Gunnison sage grouse, now considered a separate species, has lost 90 percent of its habitat and clings to survival only in limited portions of Colorado and Utah.

For the past decade, the greater sage grouse has narrowly averted being listed on the federal endangered species list. In 2004, after petitioning by environmental groups, the U.S. Fish and Wildlife Service concluded the species "does not currently warrant federal protection." But in 2010, the agency revisited the status of the sage grouse, noting that listing is "warranted," but "precluded" at present by other species facing more pressing threats.

This reprieve has served as a catalyst for action in Montana and other parts of the West. State and federal agencies have ramped up efforts to learn more about sage grouse, their habitat needs, and how disturbances like energy development affect them. In recent years, millions of dollars have been spent to conserve sage grouse and restore their habitat in eleven western states. Much of this work has involved cooperative projects with private landowners.

Some people mistakenly believe the decline of the sage grouse has been continuous since settlement days. That's not the case, at least in Montana. By the 1930s sage grouse were so badly depleted the fish and game commission cut the season to three days, then closed it from 1945 to 1951. But when I began hunting them in the 1970s, sage grouse had staged a comeback. Despite habitat loss, there were enough birds across central and eastern Montana to warrant a three-month season and liberal bag limit.

I remember my first sage hen hunt in the Larb Hills south of Malta when there seemed to be sage grouse everywhere. Caught up in the excitement of seeing so many birds, my friends and I let our enthusiasm outrun our judgment. The limit was five a day then, and before we knew it we had a lot of sage grouse stacked in the back of the truck.

These days, I don't pursue sage grouse with the idea of filling the freezer, nor does the law allow it. In recent years the bag limit in Montana has been cut to two birds (four in possession) and the season shortened to two months. Some hunters have given up sage grouse hunting entirely, thinking they are doing their part to conserve the species. But that's a wrong-headed approach, because without funding and political support from hunters, sage grouse habitat is less likely to be preserved. Studies have shown that only a small percentage of sage grouse mortality can be attributed to hunting.

A few years ago four of us made an early fall pilgrimage to the sagebrush country north of the Missouri River Breaks in north-central Montana. After a quick breakfast we walked hard for an hour, swinging east along a wet-weather creek toward a small reservoir. We had three Brittanys in front of us combing the sage: my youngster, Ollie, and a couple of old hands named Rana and Janie. That was Ollie's first sage grouse hunt and I was anxious to see how he'd do.

As we approached the reservoir a herd of antelope studied us from a distance of a few hundred yards. "They won't be so accommodating when the season opens next month," someone said. We watched as they trotted toward the western horizon, white rumps flashing in the sun.

We had yet to see a sage grouse, although we had seen droppings. Some were dried out and bleached ash-gray from long exposure to the sun, but others had a newer, greenish tinge. I declined my hunting partners' suggestion that I put one in my mouth to test it for freshness. As we walked along the shore of the reservoir we saw grouse tracks intermingled with the antelope tracks, the birds' three wide toes clearly outlined in the mud.

"Now *those* are bird tracks," said Walt, a friend from Idaho who hadn't hunted sage grouse before.

I laughed. "Wait till you see what made them."

After a short rest we fanned out and resumed our trek across the prairie. Fifteen minutes later Ollie came to a tentative stop at the base of a low hill, but he wasn't showing the intensity he shows on game birds. I walked up quickly, cautioning him to "whoa." A few yards in front of him, partially hidden in tall grass, stood a porcupine. I slipped a leash on Ollie and commanded, "Leave it." I heeled him away thirty yards, then unclipped the leash. When he showed no interest in going back I breathed a sigh of relief. Most of my Brittanys have learned about porkies the hard way.

I had started out the morning with a windbreaker and gloves, but the day was heating up fast. I had taken off the jacket and gloves a half-hour earlier and now I stopped to roll up my shirtsleeves. In another hour we'd be sweating like stevedores and looking for shade.

While I stood watching the haze dance across the prairie, Ollie disappeared. A minute later his bell went quiet. The thought of another porcupine crossed my mind and I hurried to find him. As I approached the place where I'd last heard the bell, a dozen sage grouse rose from the cover. I swung my 12 gauge over/under on the closest one and dropped him with the first shot. The others disappeared over a low ridge before I could shoot again. A few minutes later Ollie trotted toward me with his first sage grouse, a young bird that would make excellent eating.

Sage grouse don't have the explosive takeoff of other game birds, but once they're airborne they fly just as fast. The females rock from side to side in flight, a trait not shared by the larger males. One researcher recorded the average speed of males in sustained flight at close to fifty miles per hour. They are capable of flying for miles and large flocks sometimes migrate from winter to summer range at altitudes of 200 to 500 feet.

Sage hens aren't hard to hit if they flush at close range but they can be missed. I've done it on more than one occasion, and it's always embarrassing. When birds flush at a distance in a strong prairie wind they can be tricky. I use No. 6 shot early in the year and drop down to No. 5 if I hunt them later in the season.

Without a doubt, early autumn is the best time to hunt sage grouse on the western prairie. You can throw your sleeping bag on the ground with the smell of sagebrush heavy on the air, look up at the night sky to watch shooting stars flicker and die, and fall asleep to a coyote lullaby.

In the morning you might find frost on your sleeping bag. You'll wrap your hands around a steaming cup of coffee and look out at public land as far as you can see and wonder how you'll ever find a grouse in the olive-gray sea of sagebrush. With good luck and boot leather you'll find them, but you might walk farther than you had planned, lured on by the prospect of a sage grouse bonanza just over the next rise.

Judge Owen Denny Day

Last August Joe Elliott caught me off guard. "What are your plans for Judge Owen Denny Day?" he asked. He had that smug look he gets when he makes a long crossing shot on a rooster pheasant.

The electrical impulses in my brain hiccupped a few times and then began to fire. Judge Owen Denny, I recalled, was the man credited with bringing the ring-necked pheasant to America. Joe and I had once decided, over a few bottles of Black Dog Ale, the opening day of pheasant season should be a national holiday named in honor of Judge Owen Nickerson Denny.

While serving as U.S. Consul-General in Shanghai, China, in 1881, Judge Denny shipped several crates of pheasants to Portland, Oregon. Few, if any, survived. Undeterred, the next year he sent another shipment to his brother John, who released them near the family's Willamette Valley homestead. Judge Denny wrote to a friend, "These birds are delicious eating and very game and will furnish fine sport."

His words were prophetic. Within ten years the long-tailed birds had spread throughout the Willamette Valley. Oregon's first pheasant season in 1892 produced a harvest of 50,000 birds on the first day. Judge Denny, who died in 1900, lived long enough to see his experiment succeed, but he couldn't have imagined the magnitude of the new American tradition he had spawned.

Other states soon clamored for Oregon birds to stock in their own backyards. Although pheasants had been introduced on the East Coast as early as 1733, these efforts had always failed. Now, though, the right strain of pheasant had found the right conditions, and the Chinese ringneck population exploded like a Roman candle.

In the early 1900s, many state fish and game departments established bird farms to raise and release pheasants. These stocking programs produced spectacular results. By 1944, South Dakota could boast sixteen million ringnecks, and pheasants had a foothold across much of the nation north of the Mason-Dixon line.

Last year, Judge Owen Denny Day found us parked at the south end of Alvy's coulee an hour before dawn, sipping coffee. "Whose idea was it to get up so early?" I asked.

"It is pretty dark for hunting pheasants. Better to get here early, though, so no one horns in on our spot."

As usual, we started hunting too soon. In Montana it's legal to hunt upland birds a half hour before sunrise, but it's still too dark to tell hens from roosters. We always wait until we think it's light enough—but it never is—so we end up watching the first few birds fly away unscathed.

I steered my Brittany, Ollie, into a heavy stand of Conservation Reserve grassland bordering the east side of the coulee, while Joe took his young Brittany, Gret, through the lighter grass and snowberry carpeting the other side. I hadn't gone far when Ollie's bell stopped ringing. A pheasant of unknown gender exploded from the grass at my approach and disappeared into the gloaming. Much to Ollie's displeasure, I clipped a leash on his collar and sat down to wait for better light.

While we waited, a rooster crowed in the wheat stubble off to the east. Another answered, then another. Several pheasants flew from the wheat stubble into the coulee. Ollie strained at his leash. Suddenly the sun appeared on the eastern horizon, its first rays gilding the grass with golden light. Time to hunt.

Ollie disappeared into the tall grass ahead of me, his bell ringing a merry tune. I had debated whether to use his beeper collar or his bell. I knew the beeper would be easier to keep track of in the heavy cover, but I like the sound of the old-fashioned bell. I began to regret my decision when Ollie ranged too far ahead, his bell no longer audible. Was he on point or just out of earshot? I hastened forward, eyes peeled for any sign of him. Then I heard—or thought I heard—a muffled "ding" off to my left. I turned in that direction and a minute later spotted his motionless form.

When I stepped in front of Ollie a rooster blasted skyward, then leveled off and curled back the way we'd come. He folded when I pulled the trigger. Ollie quickly found him and danced toward me with our first pheasant of the season. On the far side of the coulee I heard Joe shoot twice, then yell "Fetch, Gret!" When he emerged

from a grove of Russian olives he held Gret's pheasant high for me to see.

An hour later we each had our limit of three birds. Back at the truck we sat on the tailgate and talked with our landowner friend, Alvy, who had driven down to see how we were doing. "I thought you'd get your birds this morning," he said. "We had a mild winter and a good hatch this spring. I've been seeing lots of birds in the stubble every evening since we combined our wheat."

In mid-November Joe and I paid a second visit to Alvy's coulee. A northwest wind sharp enough to slice coconuts hit us when we got out of the truck. Our insulated boots crunched in three inches of fresh snow. The golden leaves of autumn were gone, replaced by the monochrome of early winter. I knew that somewhere in the bleak landscape that lay before us, battle-hardened roosters were revving their engines and getting ready to run.

We worked the first half-mile of cover without putting up a rooster. Ollie and Gret seemed birdy much of the time, but came to solid points only twice—both times on hens. Two hundred yards ahead I could see pheasants boiling out of the coulee and flying over the low hill to the west—first a few, then a dozen. A lot of them looked like roosters.

As we moved up the creek bottom we flushed a few more hens, then Ollie skidded to a point near a tangle of wild rose. Expecting another hen, I walked in nonchalantly. To my surprise, a rooster clattered up, cackling and knocking snow from the bushes. I tried not to shoot too fast, but when he got out twenty yards I downed him with a load of copper-plated No. 5 shot.

"That rooster didn't get the memo," Joe said. "All his buddies bailed out of here fifteen minutes ago."

"A gift bird," I replied, "thanks to my clean living."

I hunt pheasants with a 12 gauge over/under choked improved cylinder and modified. I know hunters who do well with smaller gauges, but they shoot their birds over points at close range. I don't have that much self-discipline, so I follow the advice of Nash Buckingham, who said of shotguns, "The good big one beats the good little one every time." Mr. Nash was talking about guns for waterfowl, but his words apply just as well to late-season pheasants—big, tough birds that can absorb lead and keep flying.

I start the season with No. 6 shot but switch to No. 5 later on. I've used Federal Premium copper-plated loads on pheasants for more than twenty years and believe the high quality of these shells justifies the extra expense. When I hunt pheasants in areas where steel shot is required I use three-inch shells with No. 2 or 3 shot. I haven't experimented with many loads, but last fall I killed a rooster at the far edge of shotgun range with a load of Federal Premium Black Cloud No. 2. He didn't move when he hit the ground. If it sounds like I'm a salesman for Federal shells, I almost was. Many years ago they offered me a job in their sales department. I turned it down to pursue a career in natural resource journalism, but I've been using their shells ever since.

I love shotguns and have several. Hunters who limit themselves to a gun or two deny themselves one of the pleasures of an outdoor life: owning several guns to use and admire. Having said that, I think most hunters shoot their *best* when they stick with one gun. I do almost all my upland hunting with a Browning over/under I've had for thirty years. It fits me well and I'm comfortable with it—familiarity breeds good wingshooting.

A half-hour after I shot the gift bird I had reason to be glad I'd brought my 12 gauge and heavy shot. Catching the scent of the birds that had flown out of the creek bottom, Ollie made a long cast over the lip of the coulee and out into the short, sparse grass of the mature Conservation Reserve field beyond. I reluctantly followed, but I knew these birds would be running and nearly impossible to flush in shotgun range.

Working into the stiff northwest breeze, Ollie pointed briefly, then cat-walked ahead. I followed as fast as I could but I'm no match for a running rooster. Ollie shadowed the bird for a hundred yards before coming to another halt. I struggled along behind, wishing the bird would fly so I could steer Ollie back into the coulee where we might get one to sit tight. When I got closer to Ollie I stepped up the pace. As I passed him the rooster came up forty yards ahead, flying low and angling back toward the coulee, offering a crossing shot. I swung the gun well past his beak and pulled the trigger. To my surprise, he dropped like a stone.

Back at the truck an hour later Joe and I exchanged our tales of woe. Gret had pinned a rooster in heavy cattails at the edge of a frozen pond, giving Joe an easy shot. But his cold-numbed fingers couldn't find the safety. Several others laid down a twisted trail of scent and disappeared like feathered Houdinis. Ollie had trailed another bird through the Conservation Reserve field, but that one lifted beyond gun range. These birds were typical late-season roosters: hard to find, hard to get close to, and hard to kill.

Some hunters believe that pheasants today run more than they used to—that natural selection has produced a super-race of ringnecks reluctant to take wing. I doubt it. Horace Lytle, gun dog editor for *Field & Stream* in the 1930s, wrote this about hunting pheasants with his Irish setter:

> Smada Byrd would have to rate as one of the great pheasant dogs I have known. . . . Byrd pinned many a pheasant to point and made it stick tight. On others that might be

running she would put on a pretty roading performance.
By keeping up with her you'd be almost sure of a shot. . . .
Her very experience with pheasants, however, led to one
weakness: Let a running bird emerge from cover into barren
ground, Byrd seemed to sense it was a goner anyhow so she
might as well have some fun—and she'd dash ahead full
steam to put it to wing with all the abandon of a puppy,
showing manifest anger at the bird.

That sounds a lot like pheasant hunting in the twenty-first
century. Hunters who refuse to hunt them for fear of ruining their
pointing dogs are missing out on a lot of fun. Good dogs can learn
to handle rooster pheasants without losing their pointing manners.
On my last hunt of the 2009 season, Ollie made a long cast and
disappeared over a rise. I wanted to change directions, so instead of
following I called and whistled for him to no avail. By the time I started
looking for him he'd been gone a good ten minutes. Eventually I saw
him on point, so far away I could barely see him. It took me another
five minutes to reach him. When I got there, I flushed and shot the
long-tailed cockbird he had held for me the entire time. Ollie may
have been frustrated many times in two months of chasing running
roosters, but he certainly hadn't lost his pointing instinct.

Unlike Judge Owen Denny's shipment of pheasants to Oregon
in 1882, Joe's and my idea for making opening day of pheasant season
a national holiday hasn't borne fruit. But that doesn't keep us from
celebrating our own private holiday each October and proposing a
toast in his honor at the end of the day.

An Ammunition Maker's
Best Friend

———◆———

First a downwind zinger raced by and I shot behind it. Then an upwind floater tooled past, and I had the impression it wasn't moving at all. I shot behind that one, too. My gracious host, Kansan Bill Nye, grinned. "You have to get that gun barrel moving a tad faster if you want mourning dove for dinner," he said. I mopped my perspiring brow, slapped a mosquito, and made a mental note to get the gun in front and keep swinging.

Since that first dove hunt many years ago I've hunted doves in several states, including Montana, where doves became legal game in 1983. A number of northern states have joined Montana in holding dove seasons, including North Dakota, Minnesota, and Wisconsin. Doves migrate south in early fall, but a September 1 opener gives northern hunters a chance to test their skills on a bird regarded as a true test of wingshooting prowess.

Hunting pressure nationwide is intense, with close to twenty million birds harvested annually. That may seem like a lot, but the U.S. Fish & Wildlife Service estimates there are 350 million doves at the start of hunting season each fall. Annual mortality ranges from 60 to 80 percent, even in states that don't have hunting seasons. Doves can sustain these high losses because they breed throughout the continental U.S. as well as southern Canada and Mexico, and they raise several broods during the summer.

Each fall hundreds of thousands of hunters across the country take to the field in pursuit of mourning doves. Most of them cuss and sputter their way through more than a box of shells to get a limit (ten to fifteen birds), and feel proud of themselves at that. When dove season opens, ammunition makers rub their hands in glee.

What makes doves so tricky? For one thing, they breeze right along—they've been clocked at fifty-five miles per hour. But even more daunting is their erratic flight pattern, which the late John Madson referred to as the dove's "odd flickering quality." In his book *The Mourning Dove*, Madson asserts, "When a cruising dove is fired upon, it may perform amazing acrobatics in the twinkling of an eye. No other game bird has such a dazzling change of pace. I've seen doves do a complete roll in the process of turning and diving. . . . Unless one has hunted doves, he can have no idea of how agile they really are—or how fast."

I found this out for myself one windy September afternoon near Valentine, Nebraska. Two friends and I had taken stands at strategic locations around an abandoned homestead. I chose an opening in a wooded area not far from a dilapidated barn, Jon a hemp patch at the site of an old corral, and Clark a pasture at the opposite end of the hemp. It wasn't long before we had action. Most of my birds came in

fast over the cottonwood trees from behind me or came in high straight toward me. I soon had a pile of empty shells at my feet, but I also had nine doves—one short of the Nebraska limit. I wanted that tenth dove badly.

Jon and Clark had their limits and came over to lend moral support. A dove whistled by at the speed of sound. I missed. Clark grinned. A gray-brown missile twisted in over the treetops to my left. I missed again. Jon snickered. A brown bombshell came straight at me from out of nowhere. I missed the safety. My Brittany, Chief, whined. The matter finally came to a head.

Jon said, "Dave, we're hungry so we're leaving now. You can stay here all night if you want. It's only a five-mile walk to camp." Just then, another dove flitted into view. I threw my 20 gauge to my shoulder and fired, and the dove collapsed in a bundle of feathers. Everyone cheered but Chief—he was busy retrieving the dove.

Successful dove hunting requires preseason scouting, which involves driving the back roads in early morning and late afternoon when the birds are out seeking weed or sunflower seeds and waste grain. The presence of several doves perched on utility wires, fences, or dead trees during feeding periods is a good indication there are more on the ground nearby.

After feeding, doves fly to water. Because they like to land and walk around in the open where they can see in all directions, they don't like ponds with steep or brushy banks. They prefer to land, then walk to the water's edge to dip their beaks. Ponds with flat, open shorelines with mud or gravel are best. Just before or after sunset, they fly to roost trees.

Doves follow the same flight patterns between feeding, drinking, and roosting areas, so it pays to set up somewhere in the flight path. This might be a ditch bank, fencerow, or shelterbelt near a picked grain field, or a grove of trees or patch of brush near a stock pond. Doves don't have the wariness of ducks and geese, but wearing camouflage clothing and keeping still until birds are in range is a must.

Because downed birds can be hard to find when they fall in dense cover, it helps to have a dog for the retrieving chores. Most dogs like retrieving doves, and it's a good early season tune-up for them. It's usually warm in Montana when dove season opens on September 1, so I carry plenty of water and watch for any signs of heat stress.

While I've done most of my dove hunting in early fall, I've had some memorable late-season hunts in Arizona. One December evening two friends and I, and my Brittany, Chief, staked out a small stock pond near the Mexican border. As we sat shivering, hidden in a grove of mesquite trees, the sun began to sink toward the horizon with not a dove in sight.

Just as we began to think we'd picked a bad spot, wings whistled, and half the doves in Santa Cruz County descended on our little waterhole. We emptied our guns, reloaded, and emptied them again. Then it grew quiet. The sun dropped below the horizon, signaling the end of legal shooting time.

With Chief's help, we retrieved the doves, counted, argued, and counted again. One dove short. Or were we? No longer sure, we picked up our empty shell casings and headed for the truck. Somewhere along the way, we lost track of Chief; back at the truck I grew worried and began calling for him. When he appeared, a white speck growing larger in the gathering dusk, he had the missing dove in his mouth.

I hunt doves with a 12 or 20 gauge over/under and use No. 7½ or 8 shot. On incoming doves I fire the tighter barrel first, leaving the more open choke for the next shot, which is likely to be closer. On outgoing birds I do the opposite. I find that I score best when I wait until the birds are in range, then mount the gun, swing through and pull the trigger in one fluid motion. Tracking birds too long causes your arms to tense up, slowing your swing just when it should be speeding up.

Doves can be humbling, so I take along plenty of shells. The national average is two doves downed for every five shots fired. I've done better than that but I've also done worse, especially on windy days. Even long-time dove shooters have hot and cold streaks that leave them beaming with satisfaction or gnashing their teeth in frustration.

Doves weigh only about five ounces, but that doesn't detract from their culinary appeal. It just takes a few more of them to make a meal. Doves can be skinned or plucked, and the meat is dark, rich, and delicious. When I'm on a dove stand I lay my birds in the shade where air can circulate around them, rather than putting them in my game bag. The faster they cool, the better they keep. When I'm back at the truck, I store them in a cooler unless I'm planning to clean them right away.

Late on a September afternoon last fall Joe Elliott and I found a spot where doves were flying from a grain field to an area with trees nearby for roosting. It wasn't the dove bonanza we'd hoped for, but enough to provide some shooting and with luck a grilled dove dinner. I took a stand next to an old cottonwood and waited while Joe walked through a nearby shelterbelt to see if he could stir up a few birds.

When I heard Joe shoot I looked in his direction to see if a dove might be headed my way. A few seconds later a gray missile cruised into view. As I mounted my gun, the dove saw me and dipped two feet just as I slapped the trigger. The shot string whistling over its head sent the dove into high gear and I shot three feet behind. No doubt about it, the gray darter is an ammunition maker's best friend.

Don't Forget the Bear Spray

———— ⦿ ————

Several western states lump blue grouse, ruffed grouse, and spruce grouse in their hunting regulations as "mountain grouse." These birds may all live in the mountains, but that's where the similarities end. A mature male blue grouse can weigh close to three pounds, a full pound more than his ruffed and spruce grouse counterparts.

Technically speaking, the blue grouse (*Dendragapus obscurus*) is no longer the blue grouse, since taxonomists have renamed it the dusky grouse. Regardless of what you call it, the blue grouse is the true westerner of the three, with a range that extends only as far east as the mountains of central Colorado. North to south its range stretches 3,000 miles, all the way from the Yukon to southern New Mexico. Spruce and ruffed grouse inhabit forests from coast to coast across the northern United States, Canada, and Alaska, but the ruffed grouse extends farther south than the spruce.

There are places along the Rocky Mountain Front in Montana where it's possible to find ruffed grouse and blue grouse, as well as sharp-tailed grouse and Hungarian partridge, in the same general area. Huns and sharptails are prairie species but they sometimes eke out a living in the transition zone where the prairie intersects the foothills. A friendly taxidermist once gave me directions to such a place. As I got closer it began to look more like elk country but the man was right. I found Huns and sharptails in the grasslands at lower elevations, blue grouse a little higher in the foothills, and even a few ruffs in the aspen groves along a stream that burbled down from the mountains.

Blue grouse are unusual in that they migrate seasonally up and down the mountain slopes. They winter in conifers high in the mountains but in spring descend to more open country for breeding and brood-raising. When the grouse season opens in early September, family groups can still be found at lower elevations, waxing fat on berries and grasshoppers. Ruffed grouse don't stray far from their home territory, which can be found at varying elevations as long as their habitat needs are met, which typically means dense streamside cover. In Montana, spruce grouse are restricted to conifer forests at higher elevations; I've never encountered one in the foothills where I've seen blues and ruffs.

Most hunters are familiar with the distinctive spring drumming of the ruffed grouse. But blue and spruce grouse also have elaborate mating rituals, complete with vocalizations and acrobatic maneuvers. One spring I tagged along with a wildlife biologist to a mountain meadow bordered by ponderosa pine and Douglas fir, where he played an unusual tape recording: the come-hither song of the female blue grouse. It wasn't long until a love-struck male strutted into view, his slate-blue tail fanned and orange eye combs enlarged. He strutted and hooted for a time, then hopped off the ground and shattered the morning stillness with a startling wing clap. My biologist friend hadn't warned me about this, and he laughed when I nearly hopped off the ground myself.

Spruce grouse are sometimes called fool hens, for good reason. On a spring backpacking trip in the mountains near Missoula I came across a spruce grouse in the trail. He was in full mating display with his tail fanned, and showed no fear of me or my Brittany. Chief struck a classic pointing pose, unsure what to make of this goofy bird with the crimson eye combs and in-your-face attitude. The grouse continued strutting while I took off my pack, got my camera out and shot a roll of film. Chief kept pointing the whole time although he looked thoroughly disgusted at the end.

All the mountain grouse can act a little foolish at times. My Brittanys have pointed young blue grouse that didn't want to fly until I nudged them with my boot, but others have been wary and hard-flying. On my first ruffed grouse hunt in Montana my dog caught a bird that didn't get off the ground quickly enough. "They're not like the grouse back in Wisconsin," I told my hunting partner. But several encounters later I had to concede they could be every bit as wild as the birds back home.

I've hunted mountain grouse primarily along the Rocky Mountain Front west of Great Falls, where the birds share their habitat with grizzly bears. The presence of the big bruins adds a wrinkle to an otherwise relaxing pursuit. I bell my dog, make plenty of noise, and carry bear spray, although I'm aware of the fact I may not have time to use it.

In October of 2007, Brian Grand, while bird hunting along Dupuyer Creek, surprised a grizzly as it lay bedded in streamside willows. "It looked like a big round ball rolling at me with a head on it," he said of the bear's quick charge. Grand curled up in the fetal position, putting his arms over his face as the bear attacked his arms and elbows. The attack lasted only ten seconds, but that was enough to put Grand in the hospital with lacerations to his hands, arms, head, and leg.

Two years later, another bird hunter ran into a grizzly in the same vicinity. Galen West surprised a sow with three cubs in a buffalo-berry thicket a few miles north of Choteau. When the sow charged, West fired three times with his 20 gauge autoloader, killing the bear. The last shot struck the bear between the eyes at close range. Game wardens ruled the shooting justifiable, which may seem obvious, but grizzlies are protected and can only be shot in self-defense.

I watch for bear sign, especially around berry patches, and head for the truck if I see droppings that look fresh. When I see large rocks rolled over by grizzlies searching for ants and grubs, the hair stands up on the back of my neck. Once I ran into a bowhunter who said he'd been hunting three days and had seen more grizzly bears than elk. Although he mentioned there were plenty of grouse around, I decided to try a different spot.

I've yet to see a grizzly while I've been bird hunting, although I have seen a few black bears. One day while we were hunting the foothills west of Choteau looking for grouse, my Brittany, Chief, pointed on a grassy slope above me. No bird flew when I climbed up there, and as I pressed forward, Chief pussy-footed past me, stiff-legged and reading the breeze, still getting a noseful of scent. He went on that way for some time, finally locking up again twenty-five yards from a Douglas-fir thicket. This time a big male blue grouse took off and headed for cover; my shot charge caught up with him just as he disappeared into the trees. As Chief went into the thicket to fetch the bird, a young black bear made a noisy exit from the other side. Chief came back looking big-eyed and with his hackles raised, but he had the bird in his mouth.

Grouse are grouse, and mountain grouse aren't any harder to kill than their eastern brethren. No. 7½ shot is adequate for ruffed and spruce grouse, while No. 6 is preferable for the larger blues. All three species make excellent table fare. Because hunting mountain grouse often involves miles of walking in steep terrain, toting a lightweight 20 gauge has its advantages—and don't forget the bear spray.

A Lonely, Wild Bird

———◦❦◦———

There's a little town called Rothsay in western Minnesota where I often stop on my cross-country travels. It's on Interstate 94, not far from the North Dakota line. A truck stop just off the freeway serves up a mean country breakfast, but best of all, a giant statue of a prairie chicken sits right across the road from the diner. The statue is thirteen feet high, eighteen feet long, and weighs 9,000 pounds!

I visited Rothsay for the first time in the 1970s. I was working full time, but had enrolled in a night class in ornithology at the University of Minnesota. The class culminated in a spring field trip to Rothsay to watch prairie chickens on their booming grounds. "Booming" is the name given to the hollow, plaintive sound made by male prairie chickens during their spring courtship dance. We peered through a spotting scope as the males scooted around, wings spread and heads low, their inflated orange neck sacs visible in the morning sun.

Today only a few remnants of native prairie remain in western Minnesota to host the dance of the prairie chickens, but their booms and cackles still reverberate through the dawn near Rothsay. In fact, a blind five miles west of town can be reserved by contacting the Department of Natural Resources in Fergus Falls.

Farther east, in central Wisconsin, the Buena Vista Grasslands serves as a model of prairie chicken restoration, thanks in large part to wildlife biologists Frederic and Frances Hamerstrom. A Boston debutante, Frances gave up a life of privilege to become the only woman to earn a graduate degree under Aldo Leopold at the University of Wisconsin, and Frederic became the only person to earn a doctorate under Leopold. Frederic, who died in 1990, and Frances, who died in 1998, were inducted into the Wisconsin Conservation Hall of Fame in 1996 for their work in saving the prairie chicken from extirpation in Wisconsin.

The Buena Vista Grasslands, managed by the Wisconsin Department of Natural Resources, is a good place to observe the annual prairie chicken mating ritual. April is the best time, and reservations for observation blinds can be made through the University of Wisconsin at Stevens Point.

Hunting prairie chickens had long been a dream of mine, but I'd never made the trip from my home in western Montana to South Dakota or Nebraska where the closest huntable populations reside. Then one day, at a meeting of conservation specialists in Winnipeg, Manitoba, Lady Luck smiled. On a tour of a wildlife refuge I sat down next to Jon Farrar, a longtime senior editor of *Nebraskaland* magazine. It didn't take us long to find out we were kindred souls. We swapped a few hunting stories and made plans to get together for a bird hunt someday.

"Someday" came a little over a year later in mid-September, when I pulled up next to Jon's pickup at a café in Valentine, Nebraska, on the northern edge of the Sandhills. I didn't know it at the time, but Jon is an expert on the flora, fauna, and natural history of this unique part of north-central Nebraska. A copy of his out-of-print book, *Field Guide to Wildflowers of Nebraska and the Great Plains*, if you are lucky enough to find one, will set you back a pretty penny. He's also an avid waterfowler and author of a book on the history of an old-time Sandhills duck hunting club.

Hunting south of town for a few days on the Valentine National Wildlife Refuge, we found a few sharptails but no prairie chickens. Sharp-tailed grouse and prairie chickens (technically pinnated grouse) are distinct species, although both are sometimes referred to as "chickens." Sharptails are whiter underneath than prairie chickens, and as their name suggests, they have a tail that tapers to a point. Prairie chickens have a rounded tail and dark-brown barring on their sides and belly. Old-timers often called them squaretails.

On the third day we moved farther east to a private ranch near Bassett, where we parked Jon's pickup camper in a cut hayfield. We were up early the next morning, sipping hot coffee to ward off the chill and basking in the glow of a fiery sunrise. After a quick bowl of cereal we loaded our hunting vests with plenty of shells, water, and snacks, and headed toward a chain of low hills with my two-year-old Brittany, Chief, and Jon's eleven-year-old German shorthair, Beaver. Where the hills dropped off into a large meadow, a good-sized flock of prairie chickens flushed, too far for a shot. A half-hour later, in knee-high grass not far from a line of cottonwoods, Beaver pointed.

As Jon moved in, two prairie chickens flushed; he missed the first and downed the second. A minute later more birds rose from the grass and Jon quickly had his three-bird limit.

When we reached the north end of the meadow where the grass was heaviest, Beaver and Chief both stretched out on point. When I walked in, a bird flushed low and quartering left. I swung through, pulled the trigger with a hope and a prayer, and Chief soon retrieved his—and my—first prairie chicken. Since Jon had his birds, he decided to head back to the truck. I circled around toward the hills we had hunted earlier in the morning. Along the way, I saw a small bunch of sharptails fly across a ridge a few hundred yards away and put in near a windmill.

As I worked toward them into the wind, Chief tiptoed to a point. He crept ahead another twenty yards and pointed again. While I scrambled to catch up, the sharptails flushed, a little too far out for comfort but still in gun range. The bird I picked out of the flock dropped a leg when I shot, lost altitude, and landed seventy yards away. Chief marked the fall and soon came bounding back with the bird in his mouth.

We continued into the hills and hadn't gone far when Chief whipped into a stylish point, neck outstretched and right foot raised, at the edge of a grassy bowl; this time a pair of prairie chickens took flight, buttonhooking downwind toward the distant cottonwoods. I picked the closer of the two, its barred feathers clearly visible in the brilliant sunlight, and filled my limit for the day.

On the walk back to the truck I thought about the long-ago days when clouds of prairie chickens filled the sky and market hunters,

working from horse-drawn wagons, shot them by the thousands for shipment to eastern markets. A circular posted in Kansas in 1888 made this offer: "Get your gun and go hunting. We pay spot cash for all you can ship us, f.o.b., your station, packed with plenty of ice . . . Fourteen years in business enables us to pay more than any other dealer in Kansas City."

Not all of those seeking prairie chickens in the old days did it for the money. Men like Teddy Roosevelt visited the grasslands at the end of the nineteenth century to pursue them for the sport they provided. While doing research for their book, *The Market Hunter*, Jim and David Kimball interviewed an old-timer named Orin Sabin, who left his Iowa home in 1899 at age fourteen to work on a farm in eastern South Dakota. It's corn-and-pheasant country now, but when Sabin first saw it, tallgrass prairie stretched to the horizon.

Orin was eighty-one when he told the Kimballs this story:

> Teddy Roosevelt came up . . . in 1899 to hunt. With him he had a taxidermist who later accompanied him to Africa, a secret service man named Cole and a doctor. . . . Three boys and I rode down to the station to see them . . . I had hauled my red bird dog up on the saddle and held him in front of me, and in one boot I had shoved my 10-gauge double-barreled shotgun with one hammer broke off. The men came around and asked if I knew the country around there. I told them I knew it for miles around because all I did was ride the prairie herdin' cattle and huntin'. Well, Roosevelt wanted to hire me to drive the livery wagon while they hunted prairie chickens. He said he would give me a dollar a day. That sounded pretty good because I was making nine dollars a month. I rode two miles back to the ranch and asked the boss. It was OK with him, so I hunted with them, and the second day Roosevelt told me to bring my dog and gun along. I hunted prairie chickens with them for the next six days. When he paid me off he gave me a twenty-dollar bill, and I started to the bank to get it

changed. But he called me back and said, "Just keep it. That's yours." . . . When the engine hooked on the train to pull the cars out, he called me to the door and handed me a double-barreled shotgun. I looked at it and said, "Both hammers are lost." But he explained that it was a Baker Hammerless. Boy! And those were in the black powder days!

It's hard to imagine the numbers of sharp-tailed grouse and prairie chickens that graced our grasslands just over a century ago. As the prairies began to fill with settlers, the birds at first flourished thanks to new food sources like wheat and corn. For a time, when cropland struck a perfect balance with native prairie, a market hunter might kill up to a hundred prairie chickens a day. But the heyday was short-lived, as the grasslands these birds need for courtship and nesting began to shrink.

Prairie chickens melted away in many states where they were once abundant. Some states, like Iowa, successfully reintroduced them, while others tried and failed. Remnant flocks still exist in Wisconsin, Minnesota, North Dakota, Illinois, and Missouri, thanks to the efforts of conservationists. The best huntable populations are found today in South Dakota, Nebraska, and Kansas.

According to the North American Grouse Partnership, only about 10 percent of North America's native grasslands remain. Conservation groups like Pheasants Forever and Quail Forever are working with the Partnership to restore prairie grouse habitat, but it's an uphill battle. John Madson, in his book *Where the Sky Began*, called the prairie chicken's springtime booming a lonely, wild sound made by a lonely, wild bird. "When it is gone," he wrote, "it shall be gone forever. All our television will not bring it back to us, and none of our spacecraft can take us to where it vanished."

Let's hope that day never comes.

Gentleman Bob

———•❧•———

We rarely ran into bobwhite quail when I was a kid growing up in west-central Wisconsin. We must have been at the northern edge of the bobwhite's range, because when we hunted counties south of Eau Claire we would see an occasional covey, while hunting to the north we never did. Shooting a quail was cause for celebration and I only remember bagging a few. According to *Wisconsin Natural Resources* magazine, bobwhites have declined steadily in southern Wisconsin since the 1940s due to shrinking habitat.

When I worked for a time in the Twin Cities my friend Rod Sando and I made several trips to Iowa to hunt pheasants and quail. There were good numbers of both species south of Des Moines in those days. If we could find an empty farmstead with an Osage orange hedgerow, we often found a covey of bobwhites.

Rod had a reputation as an expert ruffed grouse hunter and had gotten to know some of the Minnesota Vikings who liked to hunt. One of them was the late Wally Hilgenberg, a linebacker who had the distinction of playing in all four of the Vikings' Super Bowl appearances.

Wally was from southern Iowa and had relatives in Coon Rapids, a small town in the western part of the state. Rod had hunted with Wally and his uncle and cousins in the Coon Rapids area a number of times, and he invited me to go along on his next trip. Wally couldn't get away, so it was just Rod and me.

I remember sitting in the café in town having breakfast and noticing the locals glancing our way and whispering. At first I figured we had parked illegally or skipped out on our bar tab the night before, but judging by how nice everyone had been treating us it didn't seem like we were headed for the hoosegow. The waitress couldn't stay away from our table with her coffee pot, and she seemed especially impressed with Rod.

When I mentioned it, Rod laughed. "We're celebrities, Dave. Because I've hunted down here with Wally Hilgenberg they figure we're pro athletes."

"Yes, but we're not big enough to be pro football players. So who do they think we are?"

"When Wally first introduced me around here as Rod Sando, some of the folks got me confused with Ron Santo." Ron Santo was an all-star third baseman with the Chicago Cubs, and he and Rod were about the same age. I started to sweat, wondering whose name I should sign in case someone asked for my autograph. We left a big tip and talked a little baseball at the cash register. It may have been a coincidence, but getting permission to hunt wasn't a problem on that trip. Word travels fast in small towns.

The bobwhite quail is our most widely distributed upland game bird, with the exception of the mourning dove. Its range extends throughout the South, much of the Midwest, and in the East as far north as Massachusetts. Bobwhites stretch west through Texas and into eastern New Mexico. Sadly, they have declined throughout much of their range. Urban sprawl, shrinking grasslands, and changes in farming practices have all taken their toll.

Having never lived in the heart of bobwhite country, I can't speak with authority about hunting them. But I've gone on many an armchair quail hunt with a good book instead of a shotgun. To get the flavor of hunting Gentleman Bob in the Old South, you can't go wrong by reading Havilah Babcock, Nash Buckingham, and Archibald Rutledge. For a comprehensive look at quail history, biology, and hunting, Charles Elliott's book, *Prince of Game Birds: The Bobwhite Quail*, is a good read. Joel Vance's *Bobs, Brush, and Brittanies* will teach you plenty about birds and bird dogs and keep you smiling the whole time.

The late Charley Waterman, who for years divided his time between Livingston, Montana, and Deland, Florida, wrote about chasing quail among the pines and palmettos of his winter home. Charley, who grew up in Kansas bobwhite country and hunted them throughout their range, was an expert on the subject. One November when I left my home in Helena to embark on a Nebraska quail hunt, I stopped in Livingston to ask Charley for advice. I'd never met him in person, although I'd talked to him on the phone a couple of times.

When I arrived at his house he was kind enough to invite me in, talk about quail and Hungarian partridge hunting for an hour, and autograph my copy of his book, *Hunting Upland Birds*, the first chapter of which is devoted to the bobwhite. When he walked me out to my car—a 1975 Ford Pinto loaded to the roof with hunting gear, my Brittany riding shotgun—he did a doubletake. "Say," he said, "isn't that one of those exploding Pintos?" The Ford Pinto had a design flaw that made the gas tank prone to being ruptured in a rear-end collision, ending in the fiery death of its occupants.

"Yes," I said, "but I've driven it several years without a problem." Charley had a concerned look on his face as I drove away, not unlike a worried father sending his son off to war.

I made the long trip to Lincoln, Nebraska, without being incinerated and met my friend Jon Farrar at his house. After we'd had a cup of coffee and discussed our hunting plans, he eyeballed my unconventional hunting rig. "Hey," he said, "isn't that one of those exploding Pintos?"

Jon and I hunted quail and pheasants around Lincoln for the next few days with good success. I was anxious to hunt bobwhites with my Brittany, Chief, because I had the idea I might get around to hunting all the upland game birds in the continental U.S. with him, as Charley Waterman had done with a legendary Brittany named Kelly. As it turned out, Chief and I didn't get them all, but we came close.

I figured, correctly, that Chief would quickly learn to handle the tight-sitting bobwhites, since he'd had plenty of experience with Huns back in Montana. When he skidded to a point in a weedy draw the first morning, I forgot everything Charley Waterman had told me. "They're likely to get up right in your face," Charley said,

"and they'll give you the impression they're going faster than they really are. Don't hurry too much and remember to pick out one bird at a time."

Of course, the explosive covey rise rattled me and I shot too fast. For such small birds, they make a lot of noise. Havilah Babcock, a University of South Carolina English professor and poet laureate of southern quail hunting, explained it this way: "Seven ounces of avoirdupois could be wrapped up in no other shape or form that would possess such power to befog and confound the senses or to disconcert and disorganize the human nervous system." I missed with the first barrel but scratched one down with the second. An hour later Chief pointed again near the edge of a cornfield. This time I calmed my nerves and doubled on the covey rise, a performance I repeated only once during the remainder of the trip.

My most vivid recollection came on the last afternoon of our hunt. Late in the day Jon and I scattered a covey at the edge of a woodlot, and I shot two singles over Chief's points. The third bird he pointed flew into the woods, dodging through the oak trees. I thought I saw it slant down at my shot, but I lost sight of it in the thick undergrowth. The sky was growing darker, and I didn't think I had much chance of finding it, but I urged Chief to "hunt dead." He disappeared while I scuffled around in the leaves and twigs carpeting the ground, hoping for a miracle. A cold wind muttered through the trees, sending the brown oak leaves still clinging to the branches into a nervous chatter. When I heard his bell getting louder, I turned to see him coming toward me with the pretty little cock quail in his mouth, just as amber rays from a dying sun washed across the woodlot.

While my experience with bobwhites may be limited, I've shot a lot of Mearns quail in southern Arizona with No. 8 trap loads. Like bobwhites, these birds hold tight for a pointing dog. Most shots are in heavy cover at close range, requiring a gun choked skeet or improved cylinder—a combination that also works well for bobwhites.

There are no bobwhite quail in Arizona, unless you count the masked bobwhite, a subspecies on the endangered species list. While visiting southern Arizona a few winters ago, I drove up a gravel road south of Tucson into the Santa Rita Mountains. Past the turnoff to Madera Canyon, a popular birding spot that hosts a rare, long-tailed bird called the elegant trogon, the Box Canyon Road winds upward through a narrow canyon. On top the terrain levels out into rolling, oak-covered hills, part of the Coronado National Forest. I pulled off at a roadside turnout to let my Brittany, Ollie, water the trees.

There was a public access sign at the barbed-wire fence, so I went through the gate and started up a well-worn trail to look around. Out of nowhere appeared two Brittanys with a pair of hunters not far behind. I hadn't seen a soul for the past hour—or another vehicle—so I was surprised, to say the least. The hunters, both carrying vintage 28-gauge double guns that made my mouth water, said they hadn't seen any Mearns quail that morning, but they had found them here on previous trips.

Like a dutiful greenhorn, I asked them about the trail. "It's the Arizona Trail," said one. "It goes north from the Mexican border all the way to the Utah." Then I asked them if they'd ever run across a masked bobwhite. They laughed and said the masked bobwhite lives only on the Buenos Aires National Wildlife Refuge, forty miles south, right on the Mexican border. "And down there," said one, "you're more likely to find a drug smuggler or a Mojave rattlesnake than a masked bobwhite."

HELPERS IN THE HUNT

How many dogs does a man need? He may
finally need only six feet of space, but in the
meantime he needs many, many dogs.

John Motoviloff, *Driftless Stories*

A Dog's Life

———•⟨≈⟩•———

While packing for a duck hunting trip last fall, moving gear from the house to the truck, I carelessly left the kitchen door ajar. Preoccupied with my chores, I didn't notice that my two-year-old black Lab, Bailey, had slipped out of the house. When I realized she was missing, I got the sinking feeling all dog owners dread.

I hurried up and down the gravel road in front of the house calling her name. No luck. Then, as I was getting in the truck to search the neighborhood, I saw her coming down the road. She had something in her mouth, which turned out to be an apple from my neighbor's yard. Maybe it was her way of telling me she'd be a good retriever if I took her along on the trip. She needn't have worried, since she is as important to my waterfowl outings as my shotgun and waders. Relieved, I took the apple and gave her a hug.

This small incident reminded me of how much we hunters care about our dogs. When they are sick, hurt, or lost, we suffer, much as we would for any member of our family. But then, retrievers *are* family. They play with our kids, guard our houses (sort of), give us their unconditional love. Sure, sometimes they make us want to tear our hair out, but most of the time they make us laugh. They'd be our pals even if they didn't retrieve ducks and geese.

We shepherd them through their too-short lives, just as they guide us from one milestone to the next in our own lives. Think about it. The bundle of puppy energy you bring home when you send your daughter off to first grade may be around to retrieve her first duck, check out her first date, and see her off to college.

Just as we humans pass through childhood, adolescence, early adulthood, and finally maturity, retrievers progress through four life stages: exuberant puppy, promising young dog, master hunter, and golden ager. Along the way, our relationships with our dogs change. We start out as protector and provider, progress to trainer, then to hunting partner, and finally to companion. Of course, we are to some degree all these things throughout a dog's life, but over time our responsibilities shift and our bond grows.

The First Year

I've been lucky enough to accompany several fine retrievers along their life's journey. Each has been special, and each has taught me something new. Like most retrievers, my Lab pup Bailey liked carrying things right from the start: a rolled-up pair of socks, a favorite toy, a pint-size training dummy. During our walks in the hills above my house, she brought me a steady stream of pinecones and old deer bones. I made a fuss over each prize, because it's always good to reinforce a puppy's retrieving instinct.

That instinct is a wonderful thing . . . most of the time. There came a summer evening when Bailey ran up the road near my house at dusk and began to bark. As I strained to see through the fading light, she started toward me with something black and white in her mouth. Even before the scent hit, I knew what it was: a half-grown skunk from a family I had seen a few days earlier. I panicked and yelled, "Drop it!" She hesitated, then loosened her grip. The skunk scurried into the grass and disappeared, unlike its essence, which clung to Bailey's coat for several weeks.

Like your child's first words, a pup's first duck hunt is something you never forget. Bailey's debut came on a foggy morning at a marsh in northern Montana. A friend and I put out our decoys before daylight, and then sat down to wait for the first seams of light to crack the horizon. When coots pattered noisily along the shoreline, Bailey shivered with excitement. Shortly after legal shooting time, a flock of pintails swept over the decoys. My hunting partner and I each dropped a bird. Bailey proudly brought one back while Joe's dog, Sedge, retrieved the other. That first retrieve, where Bailey's genes and training first collided with opportunity, remains a cherished memory.

Years One to Three:
Young Retriever

I got a late start as a waterfowler. I grew up hunting ruffed grouse and rabbits with my dad, but we didn't hunt ducks. It wasn't until I got out of college and joined some hunting buddies on a trip to Saskatchewan that the waterfowling bug bit. Once it grabbed me, it didn't let go. One of my friends had a yellow Lab, and after a week of watching this impressive dog work, I knew I'd have a retriever of my own one day.

A year later, I stood at the edge of a pond talking with a man about a young black Lab named Bullet. She was a field-trial washout, he said. He didn't want to sell her, but he had too many dogs. I told him I could only afford fifty dollars—I was in graduate school, just getting by. He started to walk away, but turned around and looked me in the eyes.

"Will you hunt her?" he asked.

"Every chance I get."

"Okay, she's yours."

Just like that, I had a retriever. Why he sold her to me remains a mystery, because no retriever ever hit the water harder. She had heart and courage—qualities you can't instill in a dog but can only hope are there from the start. Like many enthusiastic Labs, Bullet could be headstrong. Maybe the man had trouble with her independent streak. To her dying day, she thought she knew more about finding downed birds than I did, and most of the time she was right.

True to my promise, I took Bullet hunting every weekend, and some days when I should have been in school. My classwork suffered, but my waterfowling knowledge grew, along with Bullet's retrieving skill. In time I taught her to take a line, stop on a whistle, and take hand signals. In return, she taught me patience, and to trust the infallibility of her nose.

As writer Vance Bourjaily observed, "Hunters make errors; dogs correct them." While hunting a pond one day I sailed a mallard into

shoreline cattails a long way from the blind. Bullet's view of the bird had been blocked, but I had marked the spot well. When we got to the area, she charged into the cattails and disappeared. I figured she'd quickly return with the bird. Instead, she emerged from the cattails and, nose to the ground, ran into a grassy field adjacent to the pond. Thinking she'd forsaken the wounded duck for a hot pheasant trail, I tooted on my whistle. When she came out of the field five minutes later, she had a lively mallard in her mouth.

The next year two friends and I traveled one cold November weekend to a river in central Montana. Arriving in the afternoon, we split up to look for a spot where we might set out our decoys in the morning. Exploring downstream, my dogless hunting partners jumped a flock of mallards and winged two greenheads that sailed across the river to the far shore. Above the wind, I heard a plaintive call: "Bringgg the doggg!"

As they pointed out where the birds had fallen, sleet whipped across the water, stinging our eyes. I guessed how far the current would carry Bullet downstream as she crossed the river, then heeled her upstream and gave her a line. Landing downwind of the first mallard, her foolproof nose led her to the bird. She quickly swam back across the river with it. I let her rest a few minutes, then sent her again. The second greenhead took a bit longer, but she soon had it. That day I knew Bullet had made the passage from retriever-in-training to a seasoned veteran of the marsh.

Years Three to Eight:
Master Hunter

These are the best of years. Your dog now operates like a well-oiled machine, and the long hours that went into training are a distant memory. Possessing separate strengths and skills, you and your dog mesh into an effective, economical team—a partnership portending bad news for ducks and geese. You've both worked hard to reach these glory years, and now it's time to enjoy them.

Thumbing through my hunting journal, I found this brief entry: *French's Pond, October 7, 2004. Morning cold and clear. Paddled the canoe to a brushy island and put out a dozen mallard decoys. Good flight of dabblers until 10 a.m. Joe and I limited on mallards, pintails, wigeon, teal.*

Those were the terse words of a tired hunter, scribbled before drifting off to sleep. But looking at them now, I can recall the stellar performance of my seven-year-old black Lab, Jenny, as if it were yesterday.

Shortly before sunrise a flock of mallards passed overhead, then turned and started back toward us, pushing into the breeze. As they angled down to the decoys, wings cupped, we tumbled three greenheads into the blocks. Jenny gathered them in. As dawn broke and the sun crept over a reddening eastern horizon, small flocks of mallards, teal, and pintails came and went. Jenny kept busy with the birds that stayed behind. One mallard dropped beyond gun range and dived repeatedly as she closed in, until she trapped it in the shallows.

About 9 a.m., a flock of high-flying wigeon cascaded toward the decoys, white wing patches twinkling in the sun. They dropped around us in a rush of wings and eerie whistles, the drakes' white crowns clearly visible against a pale blue sky. Mesmerized, we blew holes in the air, managing to down only one bird.

I now had my limit, and Joe was one bird shy. While we debated picking up the decoys, six pintails arrowed in from the west, necks outstretched. A bird shuddered at Joe's shot but sailed toward a line of cottonwoods marking the far edge of the pond. Jenny swam across, entered the trees and disappeared into the alfalfa field beyond. When she reappeared some time later, she had a lovely drake pintail in her mouth. We ended the morning with no birds lost, thanks to Jenny, a retriever in her prime.

Golden Years

> Brothers and Sisters, I bid you beware
> Of giving your heart to a dog to tear.
>
> Rudyard Kipling

There comes a time when age and circumstance dictate that your old retriever must be retired because of arthritis, deafness, cataracts, or a host of other ailments. But the old dog still gets restless when autumn nights grow brisk; he rises unsteadily to his feet, tail wagging, at the sight of your decoys or shotgun. "I can still go," he seems to say, a look of pleading in his eyes. But he can't go. He may not know it, but you do. Hold him close, stroke his graying muzzle, and treasure him. He's earned your respect and love.

Before that day comes, though, there will be a time and place, before the ponds and sloughs ice up around the edges, for an old dog to join you in the field. At age eleven, my black Lab Maggie still enjoyed good health. She had retrieved most of the ducks and geese native to the northern plains, but she'd never retrieved a canvasback, the king of ducks.

I had a plan to remedy the situation—a plan involving a trip to a wildlife management area in west-central Montana. When the wind blows hard across this shallow prairie wetland, as it often does, the ducks leave open water to seek sheltered nooks and coves. On such days, a well-positioned hunter can profit.

Maggie and I made the trip in late October, arriving an hour before dawn. I pulled on hip boots, grabbed my gun, shells, and a bag of decoys and began the long walk across a dike toward the main lake. After placing the decoys off the tip of a point that juts into the lake, we settled into the grass to await first light.

As dawn arrived, I could see, in the distance, flocks of ducks winging over the marsh. Ragged clouds scudded across a slate gray sky. The prairie wind sang through the grass and over the lake, raising a chop on the dark water. An occasional squadron of divers followed the lakeshore, just out of shooting range.

Engrossed in watching a wavering line of tundra swans out over the lake, their mournful cries rising and falling on the wind, I nearly failed to see the wedge of ducks coming straight toward me along the shoreline. On they came—big, powerful ducks with white bellies, looking like silver bullets tipped with rusty red. Cans! The nearest drake dropped to the water at my shot. His head was up, so I shot again to make sure he wouldn't dive. A wounded canvasback might lead an old dog on a long, exhausting chase.

When I yelled "Fetch!" Maggie hit the water and closed in fast on the lifeless bird. She paddled back slowly, as if savoring the moment, and met me at the shoreline, holding the regal drake proudly. After a rest, we began the hike back to the truck, to a dry towel and warm heater.

Thanks, Maggie, for the canvasback. You've been gone many years, but when I close my eyes I can still see you bringing in that duck. Thank you, Bullet and Jenny, for all the good times. You were funny, loyal, brave, and smart, not to mention good at your job. I miss you. And thank you, Bailey, for bringing me the pinecones . . . and the apple . . . and for letting go of the skunk. I have a feeling great days lie ahead for you and me.

Dogs May Be Smarter
than We Think

Scientists don't credit dogs with great reasoning power, but I've had things happen in forty years of following gun dogs that have given me pause for thought. I once had a young Brittany named Sally who didn't care much for retrieving but had a burning desire to hunt. When she was two years old I took her to eastern Oregon to hunt chukars on the steep slopes above Brownlee Reservoir. She went on point in knee-high sagebrush and I bounced a bird from the covey as they rocketed downhill. Sal disappeared into the sage and I waited for her to fetch the chukar. She was gone a long time and eventually came back without it. I knew what had happened. She had found the bird, started back, then dropped it somewhere along the way—a stunt she had pulled before with other birds.

Now I had a dead chukar somewhere in the sagebrush and only a foggy notion of where to look. I was not happy, a fact I conveyed to Sal by uttering strong words of disapproval. Chastened, she walked at heel while I wandered in circles looking for the dead chukar. It took me ten minutes to find the bird, and while I was looking I tossed more choice phrases in her direction. Sal took it hard. When I resumed hunting she walked behind me. "Great," I thought, "now I've ruined my dog."

A half-hour later I flushed a lone chukar from a rocky outcrop; the bird tumbled far down the hill at my shot. To my amazement, Sally ran down the hill and brought it back. I showered her with hugs and kisses and she began hunting again. She retrieved flawlessly the rest of that day and every day from that point on. I'd like to take credit for her epiphany, but all I had done was lose my temper and chew her out. Sal wasn't a deep thinker, but something must have clicked. Maybe she didn't want to hear me say those bad words again.

When Sally got close to retirement age I began looking for an understudy, a process that led me to Ben Williams' house near the Yellowstone River east of Livingston. Eight chubby Brittany pups were wrestling and tripping over each other when I arrived.

"Take your time looking them over," Ben said. I watched awhile. I picked up one squirming fur ball, then another.

"See one you like?" he asked.

"I can't tell them apart. What do *you* think?"

"Well, how about Mr. Mustache—see the one with the orange stripe under his nose?"

"Yes," I said, relieved that I could now single one out. I studied the litter a bit longer.

Ben glanced at his watch. "Whatcha think?"

"I think I could stand here all day and not make up my mind. Give me the one with the mustache. I'll call him Groucho."

Maybe dogs eventually live up to their names. Name a dog Spike and he might end up growly. Like his namesake, Groucho turned out to be a comedian with a mischievous grin.

In his first year he was a natural pointer—a skinny, long-legged bird-finding machine who flowed over the landscape like a ghost. I'd let him out of the truck to stretch and when I'd turn around he'd be gone. Then I'd see him, 150 yards away, on point. Groucho found more birds by accident than most dogs do on purpose.

When he was young, Groucho didn't care much for retrieving. He would fetch his training dummy, but it bored him. With birds it was hit and miss. Eventually we reached a compromise: he would make the tough retrieves—the runners and birds that fell in heavy cover. But unless he felt charitable, a dead bird in plain sight would be my responsibility.

On one of his longer sojourns in a Conservation Reserve field he caught an apparently healthy rooster pheasant. He started toward me with it, but he was still a hundred yards away when he put the bird down to adjust his grip. It flew away, feathers scattering in the wind. Groucho came back, still smiling his cookie-duster smile. "Easy come, easy go," he seemed to say.

One warm October afternoon Groucho and I stood on a hillside watching my hunting partners and their setters work through brushy cover in a coulee far below. One of the dogs pointed a pheasant, which his master flushed and knocked down. When they couldn't come up with the bird, Groucho ran down the hill, found it, and brought it to me. The setter men gritted their teeth.

An hour later he worked a running rooster to perfection, pinning it in a tuft of grass fifty yards from the edge of a little lake. I flushed the bird and shot it, and Groucho grandly scooped it up. Knowing the setter men were watching, I turned to take a bow. When I looked back, Groucho had walked into the shallow water to cool off, the pheasant still firmly in his jaws. Then he dropped the bird to get a drink.

"Fetch!" I commanded, hoping to salvage a shred of dignity. Groucho flopped down in the mud like a contented pig. The setter men smiled as I waited for the wind to blow the soggy bird to shore. They reminded me, rather pointedly, that most dogs fetch birds *from* the water, rather than the reverse.

Toward the end of his career, when failing health made even short hunts hard for him, Groucho grew fond of retrieving. He carried the last pheasant I shot for him proudly, as if he knew there might not be another, milking every last bit of pleasure from the moment. I let him strike a pose for several minutes while I told him what a wonderful dog he was. I didn't remind him of the times when he was young and couldn't wait to spit out a dead bird so he could race away to look for a live one.

My current Brittany, Ollie, has a sixth sense about wounded birds. A few years ago in Arizona I put a pellet in a Gambel's quail that dropped a leg but kept flying, topping a hill a hundred yards distant. Ollie hadn't chased birds since he was a pup but he followed this one over the rise and several minutes later came back with the bird in his mouth.

On opening day of pheasant season two years ago he pointed a young rooster that flew low to the ground when it flushed. I didn't have a clear shot so I let it go. Despite its labored flight, the bird crossed a fence seventy yards away and disappeared. Ollie went after it, caught it and brought it to me, a little rooster that just ran out of steam.

Last year we were hunting pheasants in a deep, grassy draw when Ollie scented something on the breeze and followed his nose over the lip of the coulee into a wheat stubble field that stretched for more than a quarter of a mile to a county road. Still down in the draw, I whistled and called for him. When he didn't return I began to get nervous. I climbed to the top of the bank where I could see a long way in every direction. No sign of Ollie. Then I saw him, all the way out at the county road, heading toward me. When he got closer I could see he had a rooster pheasant in his mouth. He delivered this lively but broken-winged bird to me with a look that said, "Sorry it took me so long."

Another of my Brittanys, Chief, had a great nose for pheasants and a foolproof method for hunting them. Once he got on the trail of a running bird he would shadow it, pointing and moving, moving and pointing, until the bird flushed or held tight. Because of his careful pace he rarely bumped a bird, and I could keep in gun range without resorting to an all-out sprint. When a running bird decided to hide, Chief would hold his point until I had stomped around trying to flush it. If it still wouldn't fly, Chief would run in circles to force it off the ground. It had to be unnerving if you were a rooster skulking in the grass.

Chief could be brainy, almost too smart for his own good. In his second season, while we were hunting a willow and alder jungle my friends and I called the dismal swamp, I winged a pheasant that ran into the thick brush. Because of Chief's uncanny ability to track runners I was confident he would get the rooster. He was gone a long time and when he returned he didn't have the bird. Something about it seemed odd.

Later that fall the same thing happened. But this time I noticed blood on his chest when he came back. There was snow on the ground and I followed his back trail to where he had found, and partially eaten, the pheasant. The little con artist had been scamming me for fresh pheasant filets, but only deep in the swamp where he didn't think he'd get caught. We had a heated discussion at the scene of the crime and from then on he retrieved perfectly.

One day Chief pointed a covey of chukars on a steep, rocky slope above the Snake River. The birds flushed before I could get in position but I managed to scratch down a tail-end Charlie. Hit poorly, it fluttered and tumbled far down the hill and out of sight. Chief charged after it and disappeared. When he didn't come back I began to worry. Just as I was about to start down the hill to search for him, he came out from behind the rocks far below, looked up at me, then disappeared behind the rocks again. When I finally made my way down there I found him pointing patiently into a crevice in the rocks. I reached in and pulled out the wounded chukar.

Pheasant hunting along McDonald Creek in central Montana, I lost sight of Chief in the dense willows. I knew he must be on point, since I hadn't heard his bell in five minutes. When I eventually heard a single muted "ding," I moved in that direction. Stopping to listen, I heard another ding. This time I was able to pinpoint the location and I found him stretched taut beneath a windfall. I maneuvered into position for a quick shot, should I be lucky enough to have one, and this time the hunting gods smiled. When the rooster clambered up through the thick foliage I sent him back to earth just as fast. Some might question whether Chief jiggled his bell to signal me, or whether it was just a coincidence. I believe he did it on purpose, since it happened on more than one occasion. Dogs may be smarter than we think.

Bird Dogs and Buzztails

My Brittany, Chief, was on point, and I had walked past him, a little to one side, until I was ten yards in front. When no birds flushed, I turned to look back at him. He rolled his eyes up at me, then broke and rushed forward a few yards. The snake struck swiftly; the mottled brown snake rising from the grass and Chief jumping back were just a blur. I tried to yell "No!"—the one thing I can usually bellow when I want a dog to stop doing something—but adrenaline had a grip on my vocal cords. The best I could manage was a strangled croak. Nothing I could have said would have mattered anyway, it all happened so fast.

Chief came to me quickly, interpreting the panic in my voice if not the precise message. I looked for blood on his head and chest, but didn't see any. Then I noticed a tiny drop of bright red blood on the back of my hand—he had to be bleeding somewhere. I kept searching until I found the source: a small nick near the bottom of his left ear. I squeezed as much blood from the cut as I could.

Although the rattlesnake had struck silently, it had been rattling ever since. By now my hunting partner, Curt Stewart, had walked up. "Want me to shoot it?" he asked. Curt grew up on a Montana ranch and has no special love for the critters he calls buzztails.

"Yeah, go ahead." I had never killed a rattlesnake, but then, I'd never had one of my dogs bitten before. It's hard not to take it personally. It was good-sized for a Montana rattler, between three and four feet long with a body as thick as my wrist. Montana has only one type of rattlesnake—the prairie rattler, a subspecies of the widely distributed western rattlesnake. Maximum length for this snake is about sixty inches.

We took Chief back to the truck and watched him for an hour. He looked okay, so we continued hunting. In retrospect that was a poor decision, because an hour later I noticed a goiter-like swelling under Chief's chin. He never seemed to feel sick, and the swelling disappeared in a few days. My vet concluded a minuscule amount of venom had worked its way into his lymph system, but not enough to cause serious problems. Next time I won't take chances.

Chief was a lucky dog, but my Brittany pup Groucho was even luckier. His close call came at the base of a big hill west of Great Falls I called Hun Heaven because I always found a covey or two of Hungarian partridge there. But after I ran into three rattlesnakes one September afternoon in a half-hour of walking, I renamed it Rattlesnake Ridge. I'm no math wizard, but simple extrapolation convinced me there might be more. I tiptoed back to the truck that day as if I were walking through a minefield.

I continued to hunt Rattlesnake Ridge after that, but only early in the morning if the temperature had been close to freezing the night before. I figured I could get in, shoot a few Huns and get out before the morning sun warmed the rattlesnakes enough to make them active. Good theory, but I sometimes miscalculated the amount of safe time I would have.

One September morning I arrived a little late and pulled my truck off the gravel track into the grass. The day was warming up faster than I had anticipated, and I was nervous. But the Huns beckoned, so I let my Brittany, Sally, out of her travel crate, loaded my shotgun, and took a quick hike up the ridge.

Sally pointed at the edge of a draw where I had often found Huns, and a nice covey flushed when I approached. I tumbled two from the flock and Sally retrieved them both. It was above fifty degrees by this time so I decided not to push my luck. I made it back to the truck without incident.

When I got there I kenneled Sally and unloaded Groucho, my ten-week-old Brittany pup—I knew he needed to get out. Then I took off my hunting vest, put away my shotgun and had a drink of water. Groucho disappeared around the side of the truck. When he didn't come back in a few minutes, I went to check on him. There he stood, tugging for all he was worth on a big rattlesnake he had found in the grass. My heart nearly jumped out of my chest.

I wasn't sure if the rattler was dead or just lethargic from the cool temperature the night before. One thing I knew for sure—a snake that size could deliver a lethal dose of venom to a ten-pound pup. When I screamed "Come!" Groucho dropped the snake and ran to me. He seemed fine so I put him in the truck and checked the snake. It was dead.

I took my shotgun out of the truck, laid it on the ground, and stretched the snake out alongside it. The snake was a few inches longer than the gun, about four feet in all. Although it gave me the willies, I examined the snake closely. I couldn't see any wounds, blood or anything that might explain how it had died. Its tail, complete with eight rings on the rattle, was intact. The snake was cool to the touch, but not cold; it was quite flexible, as though it hadn't been dead long.

What killed it? Certainly not Groucho, and probably not a predator. Maybe I ran over it when I pulled off the road. That's as good a theory as any. All I know is that Groucho was an incredibly lucky pup.

I've encountered numerous other rattlesnakes over the years, and most have given ample warning. Not all of them, though. One cold, rainy fall day I looked down and saw a small rattlesnake neatly coiled not far from my boots. The cool weather had apparently rendered it immobile. Other rattlers have slithered away quietly or disappeared down badger holes without a sound.

Once on a spring turkey hunt in eastern Montana I heard the unforgettable buzz of a rattler at my feet, but it sounded faint and a little off-key. Closer inspection revealed the snake to be underground, beneath a rocky ledge. I must have been standing next to a den. I wondered about the sound until I read Manny Rubio's book, *Rattlesnake*, which explains that the rate of vibration of a rattlesnake's tail is determined by temperature. At ninety degrees Fahrenheit the rattle is a blur, moving at more than sixty cycles per second. At fifty-five degrees the rattle might be as slow as twenty cycles per second.

I've never stepped on a rattlesnake, but one of my friends has. He thinks he set a record for the standing broad jump, but he didn't stick around to measure. He somehow escaped being bitten. Close encounters with rattlesnakes are not new, of course. Members of the Lewis and Clark expedition had several, as evidenced by this account from Joseph Whitehouse in July of 1805 near the present-day town of Ulm, Montana: "I walked a Short distance in the plains to day . . . and trod on a verry large rattle Snake . . . it bit my leggin . . . I Shot it . . . it was 4 feet 2 Inches long, & 5 Inches & a half round." Early Native Americans, who both venerated and feared rattlesnakes, no doubt had their share of problems.

When you consider how many people live, work, and play in close proximity to rattlesnakes today (of the contiguous states, only Rhode Island, Maine, and Delaware have no rattlesnakes), the number of human fatalities is low. You are more likely to succumb from a bee sting, a lightning strike, or a fall in your bathtub. While about 7,000 people are treated for poisonous snakebite nationwide each year, only about a dozen people die. In the past three decades, I can recall only three or four instances of people dying from snakebite in Montana—one was a two-year-old child and another was an adult male who refused medical treatment for religious reasons. In more than half of all snakebite cases, the victim—typically a young, intoxicated male—is bitten while grabbing or handling a snake.

But statistics aren't comforting if it's *your* hide that gets punctured. The venom is a potent, dangerous substance that contains primarily hemotoxins but in some species of rattlesnakes, neurotoxins. Neurotoxins are more dangerous because they cause breathing difficulties.

The Mojave rattlesnake is endowed with the highest level of neuro-toxins, hence its venom is the most deadly.

Manufactured by venom glands located on each side of the head and delivered by two fangs that fold up inside the snake's mouth when not in use, rattlesnake venom destroys blood cells, lymphatic vessels, capillaries, and muscle tissue—its function is not only to kill the prey but to help digest it as well. While these toxins are sufficient to kill a small mammal very quickly, most of the damage sustained by humans results from necrosis, a painful, progressive deterioration of tissue, vessels, and cells.

The bite, according to those who have reason to know, is painful, not unlike a jab with a hot needle. You may become dizzy, chilled, nauseated, or out of breath shortly after being bitten. The venom causes severe swelling and often kills the tissue around the bite, which sometimes leads to gangrene, possibly followed by amputation of fingers or toes. I'm told if you count fingers at a snake handlers' convention, you'll usually come up a few short.

Large animals survive rattlesnake bite most of the time, but the swelling is grotesque and no doubt painful. A lot depends on the species, size, age, and condition of the snake; the amount of venom injected (this varies from bite to bite); the depth of fang penetration; the time of year (venom production is greatest in hot weather); the length of time since the snake last used its venom (the supply is never totally depleted); the location of the bite on the body; and the age, weight, and general health of the victim.

According to veteran snake collector Stephen Spawls, author of *Sun, Sand & Snakes*, "Snake bites are a confusing subject. . . . There are so many factors that can influence a bite that the case histories from two bites from the same species of snake may be completely different." Spawls points out that some people have survived the bite of a black mamba while others have died from the bite of far less poisonous species.

Dry strikes—strikes that are superficial or introduce little or no venom—are not uncommon. One study showed that one-fourth of the bites by venomous snakes fall into this category. But all strikes should be considered life-threatening until a medical professional says otherwise.

Most hunting dogs survive a rattlesnake bite, but not all do. One veterinary source estimates fatal encounters at 5 percent. This source also estimates dry strikes at 25 percent, mild strikes (pain and swelling with little systemic involvement) at 30 to 40 percent, and moderate to severe strikes at 30 to 40 percent.

I have a book called *Nip and Tuck*, written by Ray P. Holland, editor of *Field & Stream* in the 1940s. It contains a picture of an English pointer lying on the ground with someone bending over her. The caption reads, "In spite of immediate first aid, she died from the bite of a rattler." This dog was Lola, the dam of Holland's two fine bird dogs, Nip and Tuck. Judging by the setting, the photo was taken in the Southeast. The eastern diamondback, which inhabits that region, is the biggest rattlesnake in the U.S.—some of them grow to eight feet in length and weigh more than twenty pounds. That's a lot of rattlesnake.

Despite the claims of proud southwesterners, there are no records of western diamondbacks surpassing the size of eastern diamondbacks.

One widely circulated tall tale has a western diamondback from Texas measuring fifteen feet in length and weighing fifty-eight pounds. The fact is, the maximum length for a western diamondback is about seven and a half feet.

Another myth holds that a rattlesnake's age can be told by the number of segments on its rattle. Rattlesnakes normally shed their skin two or three times a year to accommodate growth, each time adding a rattle to the tail. The brittle rattles are composed of a material called keratin—the same material in human fingernails. Because rattles are periodically damaged, lost, and replaced after shedding, the number changes constantly.

Experts aren't sure why the rattle evolved, but most feel its purpose is simply to help the snake avoid being trampled by warning hoofed mammals like deer and bison to stay away. Another theory holds the rattle's function is to attract birds, since it sounds like a calling insect. In any event, once you've heard the distinctive buzz of a rattlesnake, you're not likely to forget the sound. Interestingly, several nonvenomous snakes (bull snakes, in particular), and the burrowing owl (a ground-nesting bird) do a good imitation of the rattlesnake's rattle.

If you're hunting in rattlesnake country, it goes without saying you should be careful. But don't walk softly—although snakes are deaf to sounds in the air, they are sensitive to ground vibrations. Once warned of your presence, a rattlesnake's usual reaction is to disappear into a hole or sound off with a rattle. But as I found out with Chief, rattlesnakes don't always rattle prior to striking. Nor do they have to be coiled. Remember that a rattlesnake can strike about two-thirds of its length. To be on the safe side, it's a good idea to maintain a distance of more than the snake's length.

I don't kill rattlesnakes these days. Snakes serve a useful purpose, and unless they're close to a house or a place frequented by people, I don't see much point in killing them. In some states—Arizona for one—rare species of rattlesnakes are protected by law. As far as my dogs are concerned, I'd rather not call attention to a snake by shooting it. Snakes can deliver venom through reflex action after they're mortally wounded, so I don't want my dogs running up looking for something to fetch. It's safer to say "leave it" in a tone that means business and walk the other way.

Preventive measures to protect bird dogs from rattlesnake bite may be worth taking. "Snake-breaking" clinics in which experts use live, defanged rattlesnakes and e-collars to teach dogs to avoid snakes are commonly held in southern and western states. There is also a rattlesnake bite vaccine on the market that purportedly helps neutralize the toxins in rattlesnake venom. The vaccine will, according to the manufacturer, lessen pain and reduce the risk of permanent injury. The vaccine has been in use for several years but the jury is still out on its efficacy.

What should you do if your dog is bitten? Keep him calm and get him to a veterinarian's office as soon as possible. If you can, call the vet and let him or her know you're coming.

It's possible your dog will be bitten without your knowing it. If your dog suddenly quits hunting and wants to lie down, snakebite is a possibility. The veterinary journals list lethargy, vomiting, diarrhea, shock, salivation, and thirst as some of the outward signs. Of course, many ailments could produce any of these symptoms. The best clue, obviously, is blood or swelling around the bitten area, which will usually occur within twenty minutes. But this may vary with the amount of venom injected.

The presence of rattlesnakes in the locale you hunt shouldn't put a crimp in your plans, but it should put you on notice to be careful and to know what to do in an emergency. I try to avoid snaky areas early in the fall, especially on warm days when snakes are moving toward their dens. Wearing leather boots and loose-fitting trousers or chaps is a minimum precaution, and in some areas snake boots or snake-proof chaps may be a good idea.

Has all this research into rattlesnake biology and lore made me less likely to go into cardiac arrest when I hear the unmistakable warning buzz? Nope. My pulse rate spikes just like it always did. But intellectually, at least, I know the rattlesnake isn't some sinister creature lying in wait for unsuspecting hunters and their dogs. It's just another animal out there trying to survive. I guess I can live with that.

Strange Happenings Afield

My black Lab Maggie and I were hunting along Box Elder Creek in eastern Montana when she charged into a wild rose thicket and nosed out a rooster pheasant. The bird dropped a leg when I shot but continued flying up the creek and out of sight. I cussed my bad shooting and continued walking in the direction the bird had flown. Five minutes later I happened to glance over the bank into the creek and there was the rooster, quite dead, bobbing along in the current directly toward me. Maggie looked confused but happily jumped in to retrieve it.

One sun-drenched October morning my Brittany, Chief, pointed a rooster at the top of a big hill in the Judith Mountains. Somehow I fumbled an easy setup and put some shot in the bird without bringing it down. I watched it sail to the bottom of the hill where it stalled out in an aspen grove and appeared to tumble to the ground. I hurried down there confident I would find the bird dead or close to it.

Sure enough, Chief went on point about where I had seen the bird fall and I figured he had it located. When I said "Fetch!" he dived into the brush and came out with a freshly killed *hen* pheasant. I had clearly seen the bird I shot at, so there was no doubt in my mind about its gender. While I stood there scratching my head I heard a rustling in the aspen branches and looked up to see a hawk glaring down at me. Apparently the hawk had killed the hen shortly before I happened along and didn't want to leave. After I put two and two together I realized what had taken place, but I might have had trouble explaining it to a game warden. To add to the mystery, I never found the rooster.

A few weeks later on that same hill I shot a rooster just before dark and couldn't find it, despite the efforts of two good bird dogs. I was beginning to think the hill must be haunted. We happened to be hunting the same area the next day when one of my partners stumbled across the dead bird, about seventy-five yards from where I'd knocked it down. The weather was cold and the bird was perfectly preserved. It was a nice mature rooster with half-inch spurs, so I took it to the taxidermist and had it mounted. It's sitting atop my bookcase as I write this.

Speaking of haunted places, I was hunting a federal waterfowl production area with my Brittany, Ollie, one foggy morning in late October when it seeped into my consciousness that I hadn't heard his bell in awhile. I picked up my pace and started looking for him. When I got to a fence corner where a dry ditch intersected a hay meadow, I found him stretched tight as a fiddle string below the grassy ditch bank. A rooster flushed when I stepped in and I unloaded my over/under without ruffling a feather. Ollie bolted after the pheasant, certain it would soon fall from the sky—a case of misplaced confidence if there ever was one.

Experienced wingshooters know missing an occasional bird isn't all bad, because it affords the chance to curse creatively and passionately. I took the opportunity to cuss out my gun, my shells, the fog, the dog, and the pancakes I had for breakfast. Then I moved on to the root of the problem: me. I stood there calling myself every bad name I could think of. I quickly exhausted the obvious ones and had begun working on more creative epithets when Ollie came to his senses and turned back toward me. I'd settled on "bat-blind, bird-brained bungler" by the time he arrived. Then I noticed a curious thing: There stood Ollie, ghostlike in the fog, locked up again almost exactly where he'd pointed the rooster a few minutes earlier. The scene gave me a strange sensation of déjà vu. At first I thought he might be pointing scent from the departed bird, but the cardinal rule of pheasant hunting is always expect the unexpected.

Ollie looked dead serious, and he doesn't make many mistakes on old scent. When I stepped into the clump of grass in front of him another rooster, a carbon copy of the first, sprang into the air. Much to my relief (and Ollie's) the bird collapsed when I pulled the trigger. It isn't often the pheasant gods give a bat-blind, bird-brained bungler a second chance.

A few years ago, while hunting sharp-tailed grouse in the sandhills of northeastern Montana with Ollie, I had another strange experience involving two birds. I had walked for an hour without coming across anything more exciting than a bedded whitetail buck, which jumped to its feet with a startled look and bounded away across the undulating terrain. Then suddenly, as often happens in this wide-open country, I struck paydirt. Or, more accurately, Ollie struck paydirt in the form of grouse scent put out by a whole covey of these pretty native birds.

Ollie's bell had gone quiet in the vicinity of a chokecherry thicket surrounded by snowberry, a low shrub whose white berries provide a favorite sharptail food. When I finally spotted a patch of his white coat in the brush and moved toward him, the covey exploded from the far side of the trees, voicing their trademark *cuk-cuk-cuk-cuk* alarm call. Most of the birds escaped behind the trees, but a late riser veered to the right of the others and offered me a long shot. The bird kept flying when I pulled the trigger, which surprised me, because I felt my hold had been good and I'd often scratched down sharptails at greater distances. I watched the bird disappear over a dune, still bidding me a noisy farewell.

Since all the birds had flown in the same direction, I headed that way in hopes of finding them again. After we'd gone several hundred yards, Ollie pointed near the top of a grassy knob. This time a single boiled up, offering me a clear shot, and I downed the bird at thirty yards. Ollie quickly located the bird, but instead of picking it up and starting toward me with it, he just looked at me. I thought it odd, but I knew he was hot and thirsty, so I didn't insist he retrieve the grouse.

I walked to him to pick up the bird, and while I stood smoothing its feathers and admiring it, Ollie trotted away a few yards toward a clump of bushes. I reached into the back of my vest for my water bottle, thinking I'd give him a well-deserved drink. That's when I noticed he'd gone on point again. Sharptails aren't known as tight-sitting birds, especially when they've been shot at a time or two, and I didn't see how a bird could have sat quietly through the commotion of a flush, a shot, a dog running up, and a hunter walking in to pick up the downed bird. Still . . . you never know.

I edged cautiously toward Ollie's rigid form, gun ready. Then I saw the object of his fascination, lying a few feet in front of his outstretched nose: a dead sharptail, obviously the one I had "missed" twenty minutes earlier. The two birds, shot twenty minutes and several hundred yards apart, had managed to end up stone dead within ten yards of each other. Ollie and I toasted our luck with a drink of water, then we headed for the truck.

Sometimes the Red Gods giveth, and sometimes they taketh away. On the chilly October morning that Joe Elliott and I turned our Brittanys loose in a northeastern Montana CRP field, we expected a perfectly normal hunt. I followed an edge adjoining a sunflower field, while Joe wandered off toward the center of the CRP. I hadn't gone far when Ollie hit a fresh scent and cakewalked to a point. I flushed the bird, which turned out to be a rooster, and shot it. The bird thrashed around in the tall grass a bit but Ollie soon rounded it up and brought it to me. At that point, the rooster appeared limp and lifeless. I put it in the back of my hunting vest and continued walking. So far, so good.

A few minutes later, I felt the rooster flutter weakly—just once—a motion I interpreted to be the final spasm of a dying bird. Ten minutes later I called Ollie in for a short rest and a drink of water. I laid my gun on the ground and took my vest off and put it on the ground next to my gun. When I reached into the back of my vest to

get my water bottle and collapsible dish, the dead pheasant suddenly came to life. He hopped out of the vest and took off running, with a surprised Ollie in pursuit. When Ollie made a lunge for him, the rooster launched himself into the air like a NASA space shuttle and flew toward the sunflower field.

Most of the sunflowers had been harvested, except for one strip about eighty yards wide and a quarter of a mile long. While I stared in astonishment, the bird flew several hundred yards and landed in the middle of this uncut portion of the field. Ollie gave me a confused look. Our perfectly normal hunt had suddenly taken a turn toward the paranormal.

Joe hadn't seen this little drama play out, so when we got together back at the truck, I told him what had happened. He shook his head in disbelief. "I've heard you come up with some creative excuses for missing birds, but don't you think this one is a bit over the top? I'm hungry. Let's go to town for breakfast."

Over ham and eggs and hot coffee, I convinced him I hadn't been pulling his leg. "Let's go back and run our Labs through that strip of uncut sunflowers," I said. "It's a long shot, but maybe they'll come up with my rooster." Both Joe and I had young black Labs that excelled at retrieving lost birds.

Our plan was to cover half of the sunflower strip on the first pass, then turn around and cover the other half on the return trip. When we entered the head-high sunflowers forty yards apart, I had the feeling we were looking for a needle in a haystack. We couldn't see more than a few yards in front of us, and the dogs promptly disappeared into the maze. We trudged the quarter-mile to the end of the field, where we compared notes. "Sedge has been birdy part of the time," Joe said. "I saw a bird hot-footing down the row ahead of me a few minutes ago. Maybe we'll find your rooster on the way back."

By the time I emerged from the sunflowers at the far end of the field, I was getting worried. I hadn't seen Bailey in a long time. When Joe came out of the strip a short time later, he was grinning from ear to ear. He had both dogs with him, and he held up a long-tailed rooster for me to see.

"Bailey showed up a while back with the bird in her mouth. It was pretty lively, and she wasn't about to let it go. I have no idea how long she'd been carrying it around. I wrung its neck, so I think it's safe to assume it's dead this time."

The rooster pheasant is a tough and resourceful bird indeed. One day my black Lab Bullet flushed a bird from a patch of cattails and it flew across an open pasture toward a little creek. The rooster went down at my shot but it quickly jumped up and disappeared over a rise with Bullet hot on its tail. I was surprised when after a few minutes she came back without it. When I went to investigate, there didn't seem to be any place the bird could have hidden. True to her name, Bullet was fast and I doubted the bird could have escaped her by running. I made a quick check of the creek, thinking the bird may have jumped or fallen in. No dice. Then I noticed a badger hole along the bank and when I peered in I could just see the tip of the rooster's tail sticking out. It took some doing, but I extracted the bird.

Bullet was as fearless a retriever as I've ever owned, but she nearly failed me once. I had traveled to Idaho with friends in December for a late-season chukar hunt. A freak storm had covered the Salmon River country south of Grangeville with a foot of snow. The thermometer showed fifteen degrees when we drove through the little town of White Bird, which normally enjoys daytime temperatures above freezing, even in mid-winter. Shelf ice had formed along the river, and the creeks that wander down from the high country were frozen in places.

Side-hilling along a boulder-strewn slope high above the river, I shot a chukar that slid down a steep, icy chute into a narrow creek bottom. Bullet looked down at the bird, took a tentative step forward on the slippery slope and put on the brakes. When I said "Fetch!" she took another step, thought better of it, and dug her toenails in harder. Then I did something I'm not very proud of. I gave her a little push. She skidded down the incline all the way to the bottom.

She quickly rounded up the bird but now she couldn't claw her way back up the icy slope. Upstream and downstream frozen waterfalls about eight feet high blocked her escape, trapping her in a miniature box canyon. I pondered the predicament, then carefully worked my way to a point directly below the downstream waterfall, laid my gun down and coaxed her to the edge. Teetering on a slab of rock on my tiptoes, I got my hands a foot or so above the ledge she was standing on and took the bird from her. Then I grabbed her collar and yanked. I tried to catch her on the way down, but we ended up in a heap in the creek bottom. I tried to be more careful about where I shot my chukars after that.

A friend and I were jump-shooting mallards on a warm-spring creek one snowy afternoon in late November. It was bitterly cold—about five degrees with a nasty wind—and I was about to call it a day when Bullet rousted a covey of Huns, too far for a shot. They flew in the direction I was headed so I followed. They flushed out of range a second time, and this time didn't fly as far. When they flushed the third time they were closer and I shot once. It looked like half the covey dropped to the ground. This was before the days of steel shot and I was shooting my standard mallard load, an ounce-and-a-quarter of copper-plated sixes. The wind must have whipped the shot string through the covey in lethal fashion. Only two of the birds were dead and it took Bullet ten minutes to round up the others. My partner had heard me shoot once and was astounded when I pulled five Huns from my coat back at the truck. I wasn't proud of decimating a covey with one lucky shot. I've killed two Huns with a single shot on several occasions, but never more than that. Knocking down five was just one of those strange happenings afield.

Second Chances

———————•~⌘~•———————

No living animal on earth has so much downright fun as a wildfowler's dog.

H. Albert Hochbaum

There are a couple of truisms about old dogs and old duck hunters. One is that if you are a twelve-year-old Labrador retriever, the cold, dark water of late November looks a little less inviting than it once did. The other is that if you're a hunter who has reached the wrong side of sixty, it's tempting to hit the snooze button when the alarm goes off at 5 a.m. That may explain why Jenny the Lab and I were running a little late on our way to the Missouri River north of Helena, Montana, the Saturday after Thanksgiving.

A few days earlier, it had snowed four inches, and the weather forecast for the weekend promised a cold front approaching from the north. The migration map on the Ducks Unlimited website showed increasing waterfowl activity at points north and west. The hunt had been planned carefully, the river scouted, and the little duck boat loaded in the pickup the day before. Gray-muzzled Jenny would ride in the truck cab with me, her crate in the back displaced by the duck boat. The drive to the river would take an hour; unloading the boat, stowing the gear, crossing to the island, and setting out the decoys, another thirty minutes. A check of the regs showed legal shooting time to be 7:13 a.m. A 5:30 departure should have us set up on the island with time to spare.

It would be our third run to the river in the past ten days, and so far we didn't have much to show for our efforts. The first outing had been a Keystone Kops affair that could have resulted in a few mallards in the bag . . . if the old dog had kept still when the first bunch flew over, and if the old hunter hadn't been rearranging the decoys when the only other flock of the morning dropped in.

The second trip had produced two greenheads, one a single that came directly to the decoys and another that passed overhead low enough for a shot with the modified choke of my over/under. A third bird had swung just wide of the blocks at the edge of shotgun range, and I let him pass. An air temperature of fifteen degrees, a windchill factor around zero, and a strong Missouri River current add up to trouble for an old dog chasing a crippled duck.

The drive to the river through the moonlit landscape gave me time to reflect on recent events. A year earlier, during a late-season pheasant hunt in eastern Montana, my heart had suddenly commenced an alarming out-of-rhythm beating. By the time my hunting partner could get me to the nearest emergency room twenty-five miles away, my arms and legs were numb, and I was gasping for air. I thought I was having a heart attack. Fortunately, it wasn't a heart attack but something called atrial fibrillation: a rapid, irregular beating of the heart caused by an electrical malfunction in the atrial chambers. Spending a night in the hospital hooked up to a heart monitor and an IV drip isn't conducive to sleeping, and I spent a lot of time thinking about things I used to take for granted, including hunting, and wondering what the future might hold.

During the night, my heartbeat returned to normal and subsequent tests by a cardiologist showed my heart to be okay. The causes of atrial fibrillation are varied and not completely understood—heart defects, diabetes, high blood pressure, and other medical problems can all play a part. Since I suffer from none of these, I fall into the category of "cause unknown." When I asked the doctor about hunting, he said, "Sure, go ahead. There's no point in putting your life on hold. You could have another attack, but if you sit around waiting for it to happen, you'll be letting it defeat you."

Now that's my kind of doctor.

About a month after my trip to the hospital, Jenny's abdomen began to swell, and she suddenly lost her appetite. A trip to the veterinarian's office confirmed the presence of an internal mass. The vet operated immediately and removed her spleen, along with the eleven-pound tumor attached to it. It was touch and go for the next few days, and Dr. Steve wasn't overly optimistic about the outcome. But on the fifth day, he called and said, "Jenny's doing a lot better today—she's definitely turned the corner. You can take her home this afternoon." With luck, he said, Jenny would have more hunting trips in her future.

Jenny's soft whine brought me back to the present. She always lets me know when she first smells the river, and it amazes me how far away that olfactory miracle takes place. Five minutes later, I arrived at the roadside pullout where I planned to launch the boat and got an unpleasant surprise: Another truck was already parked there. My heart sank. I had been so sure of having this spot all to myself that I hadn't bothered with a fallback plan. In the moonlight, I could see that the mid-river sandbar that had been lined with loafing ducks and geese a few days earlier was now devoid of birds. Clearly, the other hunter had rousted them as he made his way across the river. Cursing the treacherous snooze alarm, I considered my options. Several spots would take half an hour or more to reach, putting me on the river past first light.

I decided to check a side channel a few miles upriver that can be accessed without a boat. I knew that on a Saturday morning chances were good that another hunter or two would already be set up there, but I figured it was worth a try. To my surprise, there were no vehicles at the parking spot when I got there. I quickly gathered my decoy bag, shells, and gun and started the quarter-mile trek across the snowy stubble field to the channel, Jenny at heel. As we grew closer, I could hear the contented chatter of mallards, a good omen. Several dozen ducks vaulted into the air at our approach, circled once, and disappeared into the twilight. Maybe Jenny and I would get a chance at some ducks this morning after all.

Before I could finish setting out the decoys, the whicker of wings overhead told me some ducks had already returned to scope things out. I hurriedly placed the last few decoys and checked my watch: 7:15. Time to slip into the willow-stick blind, one of several I'd built earlier in the year, and get ready. I hadn't waited more than a few minutes when a duck appeared overhead; I could tell by its reedy whistle it was a drake mallard. Anxious to make the trip at least a marginal success, I took the overhead shot rather than waiting to see if he would circle and pitch into the decoys. He folded in the air and hit the water with a splash about thirty yards downstream. As Jenny charged after him, I noted with consternation that his head was up and he was swimming for the main river about 200 yards away.

The duck dove as Jenny closed in. She tried to catch him but came up coughing, circling the spot where he'd gone under. When he popped up again a few seconds later, she nabbed him, and I breathed a sigh of relief. I know the bald eagles on the river make short work of cripples, but wounding and losing the first bird of the day—or any bird, for that matter—casts a pall on an otherwise perfect day of waterfowling.

I thought about the time a few years back when I shot a drake mallard in this very channel and didn't realize until I got home and started plucking it that it had only one leg, the other just a stub that had healed cleanly above the knee. I pictured a hungry northern pike or snapping turtle dining on leg of mallard somewhere in the bird's past. Ducks use their feet in many ways—for swimming and walking, of course, but also for steering, balancing and braking during flight. The one-legged bird appeared healthy, but not rolling in buttery fat like its mates. I felt a little sad about shooting this valiant bird, but life with one leg cannot be easy for a mallard—maybe I spared it a gradual and painful decline.

As Jenny brought in the bird I'd just shot, a wedge of ducks appeared over the main river. I had the duck call to my lips when I noticed they were swinging my way. Better be quiet, I thought, and dropped the call. When Jenny saw me raise the call, she perked up her ears and began to tremble with excitement. "Sit!" I hissed, remembering how her lapse in manners had cost me a duck a week earlier. The flock was now headed straight for us, wings cupped and paddles down. As they passed over the decoys, I picked a drake and pulled the trigger. The duck crumpled in a way that told me it was well hit. It kicked its feet a few times and lay still.

"Dead bird, Jenny, fetch!"

The next hour saw a succession of mallards, mostly singles and small groups, appear on the northern horizon and arrow down from the heights directly to my channel, as if drawn by some mysterious magnetic force. I am always amazed at how quickly they can transform from specks in the sky to plump, bigger-than-life mallards hovering over the blocks when they have their minds made up to land. I'm no virtuoso on the duck call, so I love days like this when I can quack and chuckle to my heart's content with no fear of an off note sending the only flock of the day winging south.

Whether these birds had found safe harbor in the channel for many days or whether they were just now arriving from the wheat fields of Alberta, I do not know. But one thing was certain: These mallards, with their red-orange legs and late-season plumage, liked the look of my decoys. I relaxed and shot well, probably because I knew that if I missed a bird it didn't matter—another would be along to take its place.

After Jenny retrieved greenhead number five, I checked my watch: It read 8:30. The Pacific Flyway limit on mallards is seven, but we had plenty of ducks. I decided to give it fifteen more minutes, then pick up and go home. I was watching the antics of a weasel scampering along the bank, pure white save for the black tip of its tail, when a dozen mallards suddenly materialized upriver. I blew a friendly hail call. They swept low over the stubble field across the channel, wheeled, gained altitude, and swung high over the blind, white underwings flashing in the sun. A short time later they were back, this time on set wings. I took the lead drake first, saw him fold, and then swung hard on a bird flaring sharply upward. I hit the trigger as the barrel passed his head, and he landed with a thump on the far side of the channel.

Jenny retrieved the first greenhead, rested for a moment, then swam across the channel and found the second. She brought it to me, exhausted but happy, and shook water in my face.

For old dogs and old duck hunters, second chances are the sweetest of all.

Rite of Passage

While my veterinarian friend Steve Sekerak studied my thirteen-year-old Lab's X-rays, I studied Steve's face, looking for a sign of hope. I didn't see one. When he finally spoke, his words hit me like a sledgehammer. "Jenny's riddled with tumors, almost certainly cancer. I'm sorry, Dave." A few weeks earlier, a swelling had appeared under her neck, and a trip to the vet seemed in order. Steve prescribed pills to bring it down. But as the days passed, the swelling grew worse, expanding to her face. Her breathing grew more labored. Something was clearly wrong.

So, in the dead of winter, I cradled Jenny's head, trying hard not to tear up but not succeeding, while Steve put her peacefully to sleep—a brave, good-hearted black Lab with whom I had shared more than a decade of my life.

There's only one way to fix the hole in your heart left by the loss of a faithful hunting partner. A few months later, I pulled into the driveway of South Dakota's Tall Grass Kennels, the back of my truck rigged out with puppy chow, travel crate, and dog toys. I left with eight-week-old Bailey, a British Lab of mostly Irish ancestry—dogs with names like Lochmuir Bonnie and Turramurra Teal. On the long trip home, during those respites when Bailey slept (she'd already been upgraded to the truck cab), I daydreamed about grouse and pheasant shoots on Irish estates where gentlemen in tweeds and wellies shoot classic side-by-sides at driven birds. I imagined Bailey's distant cousins sweeping in after the guns had done their job to ply the time-honored trade of "picking up," the Irish term for retrieving downed birds.

During the summer Bailey and I spent many pleasant hours at a ranch pond where she learned to fetch training dummies, ride in a canoe, swim through decoys, and stay steady to shot. While Bailey swam and explored the cattails, I dreamed of duck-blind sunrises, green-headed mallards, backwater teal, and wheat-stubble honkers. By fall Bailey was three-fourths grown—not yet a finished gun dog but showing the right stuff.

Opening day of duck season in early October found my hunting partner, Joe, and I trekking through predawn darkness to a pond on a waterfowl production area that holds the same attraction for mallards and pintails that a patch of ripe huckleberries holds for bears. With fog blanketing the water, we set out two dozen mallard decoys. Before long, ducks began to return in small bunches, the sound of swishing wings announcing their presence before we could see them. Bailey whined softly, straining to see through the curtain of fog.

Shortly after legal shooting time, ducks appeared over the decoys. Joe and I each fired once, cartwheeling two birds from a flock of about eight. Bailey retrieved one of the birds, while Joe's two-year-old

Lab, Sedge, retrieved the other. A quick inspection confirmed our suspicion: pintails. Early in the season, most pintails in eastern Montana still wear partial eclipse plumage, making them hard to identify in poor light. Five minutes into the season, we each had the one pintail allowed in the daily bag in the Central Flyway.

We toasted Bailey's first retrieve with hot coffee from my thermos and pondered our dilemma. The rest of the morning would be an exercise in duck identification. We settled into the shoreline reeds to await better shooting light.

Several flocks of ducks came and went while we vacillated. "Mallards, I think," one of us would announce.

"Are you sure?"

"Nope."

Finally, the sun climbed above the horizon, scattering the mist and suffusing the eastern sky in copper and pink. A flock of mallards circled twice and then committed to the blocks. Our salvo brought down two drakes. A short time later, a squadron of blue-winged teal flitted through the decoys; we gave them a two-gun salute, but they continued on their way. Bailey gave me a confused look. I consoled her with a dog biscuit. "Sorry, girl, but you'll get used to it." Before long a small bunch of brownish ducks, long, slender necks outstretched, swept in from the east. We held our fire, suspecting more pintails. Bailey trembled with excitement but didn't break. All those summer training sessions were paying duck-blind dividends.

As the morning wore on, the fog dissipated, revealing a line of golden cottonwoods marking the course of the Milk River half a mile distant. Around ten o'clock, a large flock of mallards worked the spread, gave in to temptation, and backpedaled toward the water. Emerald heads gleamed in the sun. We dropped two birds in the decoys and sailed another to the far edge of the pond. After Sedge and Bailey had rounded up the easy marks, Joe sent Sedge for the third bird while I held Bailey back. The greenhead dove as Sedge closed in, but he trapped it in the shallow water and swam proudly back, parading past Bailey as if to say, "That's how it's done, rookie."

We poured more coffee from the thermos and sat back to enjoy the beauty of the day. Another flock of teal, flashing low and fast over the spread, interrupted our reverie. This time we spilled two from the bunch, along with our coffee. As the sun rose higher in the sky, the flights began to peter out. We scratched one wigeon from a flock that dropped down from the heavens and circled at the edge of shotgun range a half-dozen times. As quickly as it had begun, the action ceased, leaving us to wonder if it had all been just a dream. But a bagful of ducks and two excited Labradors indicated otherwise.

Later in the season there were windless days marked by empty skies, and foul-weather days filled with wingbeats. There were memorable shots and inexplicable shooting slumps, and spectacular retrieves interspersed with lapses in retriever decorum. There was good luck and bad in all kinds of weather—the lot of waterfowlers everywhere.

One frigid November morning before dawn I waded across a river channel to set up for mallards off a brushy island. Stumbling in the dark, I ran a beaver cutting through my waders just above the knee. The trip back across the waist-deep channel at the end of the day left me with a boot full of water and a dilemma. Would it be better to take off my waders and empty them before setting out for the truck half a mile away? Or should I just slosh along as fast as possible and hope for the best? I was getting colder by the minute, and the thought of struggling out of my waders did not appeal. So I began the grueling slog. Darkness fell, my foot grew numb and thoughts of hypothermia flashed through my mind. At the truck, I stripped off waders and wet clothes with cold-stiffened hands, fumbled the key into the ignition and heard the engine roar to life.

Bailey, smelling of river water, her coat stiff with ice, took it all in stride, sneezing and burrowing into her blankets on the passenger seat. We made the half-hour trip back to town with the truck heater running full blast. The next day I bought new waders, good ones made of material tough enough to withstand flying shrapnel.

On another foggy morning on the river, I heard loud splashing coming from upstream. As the mysterious sounds grew louder, the tension heightened. A deer? Another hunter? The Loch Ness monster? Bailey had her hackles up, and I had a firm grip on her collar. Three river otters suddenly emerged from the fog and porpoised through the decoys, chirping messages to one another in a language known only to others of their kind. I don't remember if I shot a duck that day, but the otters remain etched in my memory.

On the morning after Thanksgiving, Bailey and I took Jenny's ashes to the river. Jenny had been put to sleep the previous January, and January in Montana is no time for burying a dog. Cremation seemed the best option, so Jenny's remains went down the road to a pet crematory called All Paws Great and Small. Her ashes had resided in their tin box on my reloading bench for the better part of a year, and now it was time for a final farewell.

I'd kept the ashes all those months because I wanted to spread them during the duck season, at a place on the river where Jenny and I had shared some memorable hunts. Setting out my two dozen mallard decoys—eighteen on the river side of a willow-covered point that tapers to a sandbar and the rest in the shallow backwater—I thought about the time I winged a greenhead that made it to the middle of the river. The temperature that December morning had been close to zero with a strong north wind spitting snow. Jenny fought the dark current for what seemed like an eternity to bring the bird in, and when she reached shore well downriver, her eyes were nearly frozen shut. After I held my hand over them to thaw the ice, she rolled in the snow, ready to go again.

A hen mallard quacked downstream, snapping me out of my reverie. Bailey shivered with excitement and leaned hard against my leg. "Let's hope I shoot better today, Bail."

When I took the tin box from my shooting bag, a check of my watch showed five minutes until legal time. Duck wings suddenly hissed overhead; a dozen mallards hovered briefly over the decoys before seeing us standing at the water's edge. I scattered Jenny's ashes in the wind, and the purling river gathered them in. It had already been a good season, and the rising dawn held promise for a new day.

PEOPLE AND PLACES

God doesn't count the hours you spend afield
with friends.

Gene Hill, *A Hunter's Fireside Book*

A Nose for Valley Quail

I was jinxed, hoodooed, skunked, and snakebit. Over the years I had bagged bobwhite, scaled, Gambel's, Mearns, and even mountain quail. But valley quail (also called California quail) had eluded me, despite the fact that the birds are abundant in parts of Idaho and Oregon where I'd often hunted. In my defense, I'd spent most of my time in those states hunting chukar partridge, which typically live higher up on the rocky slopes than valley quail. But it had begun to get embarrassing. School kids were shooting limits of valley quail in the farmlands around Weiser, Idaho, where I often headquartered on my chukar hunts, and I couldn't find a single bird, let alone shoot one.

I finally figured out how to do it—not through scientific analysis or boot leather, but by following a tall, lean guy named Mike Mosolf. A former college football quarterback, Mike can chase his wideranging English pointer, Sky, through rough terrain all day and hardly break a sweat.

Simply put, Mike has a nose for valley quail, and so does Sky. Because we often hunted chukars together, he eventually took pity on me. Or maybe he just got tired of my whining. One day as we drove our trucks along the Snake River on the way to a chukar hunting spot, we passed a brushy hillside. Mike pulled off to the side. When I drove up behind him, he said, "See that little draw right there? There's usually a covey of quail in it. Why don't you give it a try and I'll go down the road a bit farther and see what I can find."

The draw didn't look any different than a dozen others we had passed, but I wasn't about to second-guess Mike. I started up the steep hillside with my Brittany, Groucho, and we hadn't gone far when Groucho pointed into a brushy tangle. Soon a quail buzzed out, followed by a dozen more. I slipped on the steep slope and didn't get off a shot. The birds flew out of sight up the draw.

Groucho ran ahead and I struggled up the slope after him. When I'd gone about a hundred yards, I stopped to listen. I couldn't hear Groucho's bell, so I knew he must be on point. I'd passed a little side draw on the way up, and I wondered if the quail had peeled off into it. I worked my way around, approaching it from above, and sure enough, I spotted a patch of Groucho's white coat gleaming in the sunlight. I whistled softly to let him know I was on the way.

The first quail zipped out from under a sage bush and promptly darted behind a boulder. A second bird boiled out of the same bush and pitched downhill. I shot over him, and began to wonder if I'd ever break my jinx.

Five minutes later Groucho slid to a point near a clump of rabbitbrush. This time the bird was silhouetted against the sky when

it flew, offering a good shot. I breathed a sigh of relief when I saw it fall. Groucho retrieved my first valley quail and I took a moment to admire its teardrop plume and the pretty scaled pattern on its breast. We worked the area methodically for the next half-hour and Groucho pointed six more quail, four of which ended up in my game vest.

Valley quail have a reputation for running, especially in open terrain, but once a covey is broken up the singles hold tighter than ticks. Some hunters recommend waiting for a time after scattering a covey to let the quail move around a little and give off scent. I've never had that kind of patience. But I do know it pays to go slow and investigate every possible hiding place.

Because the majority of shots are taken at close range, I like a light, open-choked gun with No. 7½ or No. 8 shot. In open desert country where longer shots are possible, a double-barrel choked improved cylinder / modified is a good combination. A dog is indispensable for locating tight-sitting singles and retrieving downed birds.

I was surprised to learn that valley quail are not native to much of the Pacific Northwest where they now thrive, including the area where I shot my first one. According to the late A. Starker Leopold, eldest son of Aldo and author of *The California Quail*, trapping and transplanting efforts began as early as the 1860s and continued well into the 1900s. As a result, valley quail are now found in much of Washington, Oregon, and Nevada, and smaller portions of Idaho and Utah.

While the bobwhite quail has always been the darling of American upland bird hunting literature, the valley quail, too, has had its devoted followers over the years. Legendary dog trainer Charlie Babcock, who handled the pointer Manitoba Rap to a National Field Championship in 1909 (the first pointer to be accorded that honor), considered the valley quail "America's greatest game bird." I've seen old photos of Manitoba Rap, and Mike Mosolf's pointer, Sky, looks like he could be a descendant of that famous dog.

In the 1950s and 1960s, Ted Trueblood wrote glowing accounts of chasing valley quail with his pointers Joe and Rip near his home in southwestern Idaho. One of his articles he titled "Very Easy Birds to Miss." In another story called "A Day on Fluster Flat," Trueblood confessed to being totally discombobulated by valley quail, for the only time in all his experience with a smoothbore gun. "I was flustered and my dog was flustered," he wrote. "I had to call him in, sit down, and smoke a pipe before I could resume hunting with some degree of sanity."

In more recent times, author Worth Mathewson, who grew up in Virginia, wondered if any bird could replace the bobwhite in his heart. In his book *Best Birds* he concludes, "After moving to the West . . . I sure didn't have to look far. The valley quail has made its own tradition out in the sagebrush."

Mike and I have had several memorable valley quail hunts but the one that stands out in my mind took place in the Owyhee River country of southwestern Idaho. We had been chukar hunting farther north in the steep hills above Brownlee Reservoir, but a freezing rain had left the slopes ice-covered and dangerous. Mike suggested we shift operations to lower and drier country. The next morning, after driving south for a few hours, we passed through a small burg and continued down a gravel road that followed a small creek. We pulled into the driveway of a farmhouse and knocked on the door. No one answered.

"Now what?" I asked.

"No problem," said Mike. "There's public land just down the road. Let's go hunting."

"Wait a minute," I replied. "If it's public land, why did we even bother to ask?"

"People are a little edgy out here with Claude Dallas on the loose."

Claude Dallas was a self-styled mountain man who killed two Idaho game wardens in Owyhee County in 1981 and eluded capture for almost a year. He was charged with first-degree murder, but a sympathetic jury (go figure) convicted him on a lesser charge of involuntary manslaughter. In 1986 he escaped prison and went on the lam for another year before being captured again. All told, he served twenty-two years of a thirty-year sentence and was released in 2005.

We drove along the creek for a few miles, pulled over and unloaded Sky and my Brittany, Groucho. We found a place to cross the creek and hiked to the top of a small, sage-covered hill. At that point Mike headed downstream and I went upstream. I hadn't gone far when Groucho struck scent and slowed to a point. I hustled ahead and flushed a huge covey of quail, the roar of their wings shattering the still morning air. For six-ounce birds, they make a lot of noise when they take off in a bunch. I managed to knock down one bird on the covey rise, which Groucho gathered up and brought to me.

I continued walking in the direction the birds had flown, through a series of small hills cloaked in pungent sage and sparse, knee-high grass. Before long, Groucho feathered to another point. This time two quail skittered out of the grass, offering a good chance for a double. The first bird collapsed in a puff of feathers but the second escaped my load of 7½ shot.

For the next hour I wandered through what can only be described as wingshooting nirvana: The cool, damp air provided perfect scenting conditions for Groucho, the quail held tight, and my 20 gauge Browning over/under found its mark more often than not. All too soon, I had a limit of quail nestled in my hunting vest. I heard lots of shooting coming from Mike's direction, so I knew he and Sky had also found their little piece of heaven.

Back at the trucks, we laid out two limits of lovely quail and took pictures to document our dream hunt. When we were done taking photos, I asked Mike, "How do you do it?"

"Do what?"

"Find these little rascals."

Mike shrugged. "They're usually close to water, although after fall rains they can be about anyplace. I just walk until I find 'em."

Personally, I think he has a nose for valley quail.

Longtails and Liars

———————◆~◆~◆———————

I think enough time has passed that I can tell this story without fear of electronic surveillance or a full-press audit from the IRS. Some forms of gambling are illegal, but judging by the number of office pools in progress during the NCAA basketball tourney, authorities look the other way when it comes to low-stakes wagers among friends. Wagers, for instance, like who can bag the rooster with the longest tailfeather on opening weekend of pheasant season.

For several years some of the boys staying in the little public campground at the edge of Plentywood, Montana, had such a bet when the season opener rolled around. Most years it was just me, my hunting partner Joe, a couple of friends from Missoula, and the Mueller brothers from Wisconsin. We'd each throw five dollars in the pot and the winner would buy refreshments at the pizza joint in town. It was innocent enough; bragging rights were all that really mattered.

The Mueller brothers, Bud and Bob, traveled first-class in a Chevy Suburban with their German shorthairs, Gunnar and Heidi.

They brought a wall tent with a cozy wood stove and always had a cold beer and a good cigar on hand. The Missoulians, Mike O'Brien and Danny Lee, were part-time fishing guides, part-time carpenters, and most-time hunting and fishing bums. Red-haired, bushy-bearded Mike stood north of six feet tall, while his sidekick Danny topped out at about five-four. They traveled in tandem, Danny in a 1980s-era Toyota pickup with a homemade camper, and Mike in an old Dodge diesel pickup camper. Vehicle problems were not unusual for Mike and Danny, so caravanning had its advantages.

One year on the day before pheasant season opened we were sitting in front of our tents soaking up the afternoon sun when a sleek black Ford Explorer pulled into the campground. Bud Mueller was the first to recognize the lone occupant. "Hide the beer and cigars," he said. "It's FBI Frank."

FBI Frank had appeared in camp one day the previous fall, asking directions to Brush Lake. One thing led to another and before we knew it Frank had weaseled a cold beer and a cigar from the Muellers and launched into a windy brag-fest on his pheasant hunting skills. Before he left for the Sherwood Inn in town, our new friend, who claimed to be an FBI agent from Chicago, had wormed his way into our little tailfeather contest.

Worst of all, he had won . . . sort of. He had showed up late in the afternoon on Sunday with a tailfeather that measured twenty-six inches. It smelled faintly of cigarette smoke and we figured some dusty stuffed pheasant in one of the local watering holes was now missing a tailfeather, but we couldn't prove it. We foolishly hadn't specified the feather had to be attached to a bird to be legal, but that didn't keep us from asking questions.

Frank's blow-by-blow account of the day's exploits rang a little hollow, and as near as we could tell Frank was a dogless hunter. No doubt about it—we trusting Montanans had been snookered. After he left with our money we agreed a rules change was in order—from now on a winning tailfeather would have to arrive in camp with the bird attached.

So, when this year's conversation with FBI Frank inevitably turned to the tailfeather contest, Bud Mueller was ready: "Okay, but this time the tailfeather comes along with the bird, or no dice."

"Twenty bucks up front," chimed in his brother Bob, "and double on a tail over twenty-five inches." I swallowed hard, wondering what had happened to our comfortable five-dollar bet. Mike and Danny exchanged surprised glances, but nobody spoke a word in dissent.

FBI Frank did his best to look hurt, but reached for his wallet just the same. "Fine with me," he said. "I've got a line on a widow's place out at Antelope where the birds never get hunted. They're dying of old age out there," he said. With that he jumped in his SUV and left in a swirl of dust.

"If he's an FBI agent I'm a brain surgeon," said Bud. "He looks more like a mafia guy who's been relocated in the witness protection program."

"Where am I going to find forty bucks if he shows up with a twenty-five-inch tailfeather?" asked Danny.

"Don't worry," I said, "I have a feeling this is going to be your year." But if the truth were known, I was concerned. Danny had been mired in a lousy run of luck. His truck had broken down on the trip east from Missoula and he'd spent a good chunk of money getting it fixed.

On opening morning we gathered in the Muellers' wall tent for coffee in the pre-dawn darkness, then dispersed to our respective hunting spots. Joe and I hunted the Frenchman's Conservation Reserve fields out by Westby near the North Dakota line, while the Muellers tried their luck at a landowner friend's place south of town. Mike and Danny hunted the public land at Medicine Lake Wildlife Refuge.

Joe's young Brittany, Robin, went on a pheasant-chasing tear first thing in the morning, but settled down and made some nice points later on. My eight-year-old Brittany, Groucho, an old hand at the pheasant game, performed his usual magic and I had my limit of three birds by 9 a.m.

Back at camp that afternoon we compared notes. Bob and Bud had taken five roosters, but had quit early when Gunnar got friendly with a porcupine. They were still probing his muzzle for quills with a needle-nose pliers, much to Gunnar's dismay.

Mike had thrashed through the cattails bordering a waterfowl production pond with his golden retriever, Max, and limited out by mid-morning. Danny had had a rough go. His thirteen-year-old springer spaniel, Katie, hurting from arthritic hips, couldn't push through the thick cover anymore. They'd poked around and flushed a few hens, and Danny had missed a passing shot at a rooster that had flown his way.

All of our birds were young-of-the-year, and therefore distinctly tailfeather-challenged. We saw no sign of FBI Frank, but at the gas station in town we heard he'd hired a local guide.

As is always the case, on the second day of the season, hunting got tougher. The pheasants had been rousted from their usual haunts and the survivors had earned overnight diplomas in Evasive Tactics 101. Joe and I could account for only a bird apiece by noon; the day was warming up so we went back to camp for lunch.

The rest of the crew was already there when we arrived, except for Danny. They told us he had bagged a nice bird—a mature rooster with sharp spurs and a twenty-four-inch tail. But the wing-tipped bird had led Katie on a merry chase, and the excitement of running it down had given her some sort of seizure. Danny was at the veterinarian's office having her checked out. She seemed okay, Mike said, but her hunting days were clearly numbered.

While we were eating lunch, a landowner friend from Medicine Lake stopped by to say hello. Jon is a breeder of black Angus cattle, wheat farmer, card player, musician, and all-around good guy. As we were rehashing the morning's events for him, FBI Frank's black Ford Explorer rolled into the campground. He got out and pulled a rooster with a very long tail from the back of the SUV.

"Better check it for tire tracks," said Bud.

"Nope, I took it crossing at sixty-five yards with a load of copper-plated fives," boasted FBI Frank. "You don't get any closer to a smart old bird like this one. Who wants to do the measuring honors?"

Missoula Mike plucked the longest tailfeather and applied the tape measure. "Twenty-five and a half inches," he said.

"No one's going to beat this rooster," said Frank. "What do you say we settle up right now?"

"Quitting time this afternoon," Mike replied. "That's the rule."

"Okay, see you then." FBI Frank jumped in the Explorer and roared away.

"Who's that guy?" asked our landowner friend, Jon. Bob and Bud tag-teamed in telling the story of last year's questionable tailfeather.

"I was sure hoping Danny's bird would hold up," said Mike. "First he has to get his truck fixed, then Katie has a seizure—I know he's short of cash. Poor Katie deserves to spend her golden years on the couch. George Clymer's got a litter of springers coming in about a month, and I know Danny's been talking to him about one of the pups. The tailfeather money would make a nice down payment. Danny and I figured we'd row George down the Blackfoot River a day or two to make up the difference."

Jon hadn't said anything while we explained our dilemma, but now he spoke. "There are a couple of big old roosters in the shelterbelt just west of my house. We usually reserve the shelterbelt for the kids, but they're in Culbertson today. Those two roosters—we call them Fatty and Tubby—are getting downright feisty—one of 'em put the run on the cat the other day. It wouldn't hurt to teach them some manners. Bring Danny out about three o'clock."

When we turned in the driveway to the Angus ranch later that afternoon, Jon barked orders like a drill instructor. "Bob, you and Bud go down the middle of the shelterbelt. Dave, you and Joe each take an edge. We'll post Danny at the far end and Mike can back him up. We'll see if Fatty and Tubby are in the shelterbelt today. No dogs for this operation; the less noise we make, the better."

When we neared the end of the shelterbelt, things began to happen. First a covey of Huns roared up and away, then two hen pheasants clattered through the branches. When I stopped for a moment to listen for the telltale sound of pheasants scuttling through the grass, a hen exploded under my feet. I just about jumped out of my boots. For a few seconds, quiet prevailed. Then two big roosters, tails flowing, flailed skyward, cackling their displeasure.

"Take 'em, Danny!" yelled Jon. Danny's 20 gauge Remington Wingmaster pump barked once, and the first rooster hit the grain stubble adjacent to the shelterbelt with a satisfying thump. Danny didn't shoot again.

We gathered in a circle and gazed down in awe at the stricken Tubby. Or was it Fatty? The bird had long, sharp spurs and a whopper of a tail. For a moment, no one spoke. Then Mike exploded. "Now that's a *ROOSTER!*"

FBI Frank was waiting when we pulled into the campground just as the setting sun began bathing the western horizon in fiery shades of red and orange. He looked like a fox about to pounce on a flock of chickens.

"Hi, boys," he chirped. "For a minute I thought you might have skipped town. Everyone got their wallet?"

"Yeah, we have our wallets," said Bud, "but Danny got a rooster this afternoon that just might put yours in the shade. Let's find out."

Missoula Mike retrieved the magnificent Tubby from the back of the truck where he had been lying in repose. He carefully extracted the tailfeather and applied the tape. "Twenty-seven inches on the nose," he announced. "Looks like we have a winner!"

Speechless for once, FBI Frank turned on his heel to leave.

"Hold it," said Bob, "A tail over twenty-five inches pays double, remember?"

"Double on the longtail," affirmed Bud, a note of finality in his voice.

Frank hesitated, appeared to measure the distance to his SUV, then thought better of it. He turned around, grudgingly plucked a second twenty dollar bill from his wallet and threw it on the picnic table. The rest of us reached for our wallets and added to the stash. Frank stomped off toward his Explorer, his face as red as a rooster's cheek patch. "See you next year," he sputtered.

But FBI Frank didn't show up in the campground the next year, or in any of the succeeding years. Danny's springer pup, which he named Angus, turned out to be a crackerjack pheasant dog, and the six of us resumed our friendly five-dollar bet. We took some fine roosters as time went on, some of them no doubt descendants of the revered Tubby, but none of them possessed his prodigious posterior appendage. Tubby was the bird of a lifetime, and no one appreciated that fact more than Danny Lee.

Taking One for the Team

---•⟨∾⟩•---

The other day I was digging around in the desk drawer where I put things I can't bring myself to throw away and I ran across an old birthday card from a couple with whom I bird hunted for many years. Printed in England, the card features a drawing of a scowling Englishman decked out in hat, shooting coat, breeches, and knee-high boots. A ring-necked pheasant is perched on the barrels of his side-by-side, and several other pheasants are attacking his sandwiches, which are lying on the ground next to a thermos. Inside it says "Happy Birthday to a Good Sport," signed "Hen Sluicer and Horn Blower."

For a number of years this couple sent me birthday cards signed in similar fashion—I wish I had kept them all. I'm not sure how "Hen Sluicer"—the female half of the duo—got her name, since to the best of my knowledge she never ground-sluiced a hen pheasant or any other game bird. She did just fine shooting her pheasants, grouse, and partridge on the wing. I can't say the same for her husband, Horn Blower, a portly, gray-whiskered chap who lowered the boom on fast-running desert quail whenever he got the chance.

For several years we teamed up to chase pheasants and other game birds through the fields and prairies of central and eastern Montana. One November morning, on a combination deer and bird hunt near Winnett, we had just left the truck with our rifles when we spotted a flock of forty sharptails gliding into an alfalfa field. Bird hunters at heart, we hurried back and got our dogs and shotguns. After two unsuccessful attempts at getting within shooting range of the jittery birds, we decided to try a dogless ambush.

We held a brief powwow and decided, by a two-to-one vote, that Horn Blower and I, being the more experienced wingshots, would hide in a coulee and wait while Hen Sluicer would circle around, crawl along an irrigation ditch to a point opposite us, and flush the birds in our direction. Anticipating a protest, Horn Blower took the offensive. "Sometimes you need to make a small sacrifice for the good of the team," he puffed. I nodded in agreement.

"Driven grouse, right here in Montana," crowed Horn Blower, as Hen Sluicer began the long crawl down the irrigation ditch. "No need to cross the big pond to Scotland." Indeed, our plan unfolded perfectly, until it came time to make the sky rain sharptails. When the flock of grouse passed over we jumped up and emptied our guns. I don't know about Horn Blower, but I had trouble getting the barrels of my over/under moving fast enough.

As they say in suspense stories, an ominous silence ensued. Then Hen Sluicer, still plucking cactus spines from her knees and out of breath from her exertions, came wheezing up.

"How many did you get?" she demanded.

While I inspected an anthill, Horn Blower tried to blow a little smoke. "They were too high by the time they came over. . . ."

"B.S.," she interrupted. "They flew right over you, and you two sorry excuses for bird hunters didn't even draw a feather!"

That pretty well let the air out of Horn Blower's bagpipes, and I felt a cold breeze blow up my kilt as well. In an effort to repair the fractured morale of Team Sharptail, we were very solicitous of Hen Sluicer's every whim for the rest of the morning—and that may have had something to do with what happened next.

We decided to go to town for a bite to eat, then try some pheasant hunting in the afternoon. After lunch we found a ranch that had a stretch of creek bottom that looked perfect for pheasants—tall grass and shrubs along the meandering creek, cottonwood and box elder trees for shade, and buffaloberry thickets for shelter. As we drove along the county road, a rooster scuttled out of the ditch and crossed in front of us, always a good omen. When we pulled into the lane leading to the ranch house, an old dog limped out to meet us.

Many ranch dogs in Montana are of the "blue heeler" variety—they're actually Australian cattle dogs, but blue heeler rolls more easily off the tongue, so that's what most folks call them. They're useful for herding cattle, but that's where their virtues end—they're gimlet-eyed little misanthropes with a taste for leg of bird hunter tartare.

When you have no choice but to deal with a snarling heeler, it's best to throw the truck door open and walk briskly toward the ranch house. Any sign of fear or hesitation will be taken as an invitation to use your Achilles tendon as a chew toy. Out of the corner of your eye you will want to keep a close watch astern, because heelers are called heelers for a reason. Their modus operandi involves darting up behind unsuspecting bovines and applying a painful nip at their ankles—or in the case of pheasant hunters, a flesh-shredding bite.

None of us was exactly jumping out of the truck to go knock on the door of the ranch house, even though this particular heeler looked like a candidate for a canine rest home. Horn Blower was first to break the silence. "Dave, why don't you run up there and sweet-talk these good folks to see if we can't get permission to exercise their ringnecks this afternoon."

"Because, if you recall, I was the one who asked permission at the Turbitt place this morning—so it's your turn."

Horn Blower sighed. Then he turned to Hen Sluicer, who was digging a cactus sliver from the heel of her hand with the point of her pocketknife. "Hen, be a good lass and. . . ."

She cut him off with a withering look. "Sometimes you need to make a small sacrifice for the good of the team," said Hen Sluicer, her voice dripping sarcasm. I nodded in agreement.

Out of options, Horn Blower made the sign of the cross, opened the door and, with a sidelong glance at the heeler, made his way to the back porch and knocked on the storm door. Eventually the door opened partway and a white-haired gentleman engaged Horn Blower in conversation.

While all this was going on, the geriatric heeler had been gimping his way toward the porch. Then, in slow motion, he shuffled up the steps and clamped his jaws on Horn Blower's left ankle. To our amazement the two men continued talking as if nothing had happened, except for an occasional surreptitious shake of the left leg by Horn Blower, the kind of move you or I might make after stepping in a fresh cow pie.

Perhaps, we speculated from the safety of the truck cab, the rancher had left his glasses in the kitchen, or maybe he couldn't see what was going on with the partially open storm door blocking his view—at least that would explain *his* indifference. But what about Horn Blower? The heeler had been latched onto his ankle for a good five minutes, and we expected to see a puddle of blood forming on the porch.

Eventually the men bid farewell, the storm door closed, and Horn Blower gave one final, mighty shake of his leg, dislodging his tormentor, who slunk down the steps and wandered off toward the barn.

By the time Horn Blower hobbled back to the truck, Hen Sluicer and I had a case of the giggles.

"That damned old dog had ahold of my boot, but he didn't have any teeth!" said Horn Blower, slumping wearily into the driver's seat. "He sure tried gumming me to death though!"

Hen Sluicer snickered. "Why didn't you say something?"

"The guy's got pheasants up the wazoo and he was really friendly. He said we could hunt his creek bottom, and I didn't want to ruin everything by kicking ol' Gummer."

Hen Sluicer regained her composure long enough to ask, "Is that what you boys call taking one for the team?"

We were laughing so hard as we drove down the lane I thought the truck might tip over.

And we sometimes wonder why landowners shake their heads in bewilderment at us city folks.

Conjugal Bliss

I was looking out my office window in Helena, Montana, watching it snow when the phone rang.

"Hello."

"Dave, it's Joe. You aren't gonna believe this."

"Believe what? Where are you?"

"I'm on my cell phone. I'm sitting here looking at the Conservation Reserve field we hunted last opening day."

"Don't tell me—there are pheasants running all over the place, big old roosters thumbing their beaks at you."

"Nope. There is no Conservation Reserve field! There's nothing but white as far as I can see. And there are no pheasants."

"Whaddaya mean? Some of that grass was chest high and so thick we could hardly get through it. What happened?"

"Uncle Fred says an ice storm flattened it. Then it snowed two feet and the wind blew hard for two days. His power was out for over a week. He figures there are hundreds of dead pheasants under the drifts."

"Go ahead, break my heart," I sighed.

Last fall we had stumbled onto pheasant heaven. But the road had been a long and winding one. First we got the bad news from the landowner whose place we'd hoped to hunt on opening weekend. We had called a couple of weeks early to line up permission, only to find we'd been aced out. "Sorry, guys," he said, "I'm booked solid for the first three days. After that you're welcome to hunt. If you want to hunt opening weekend next year, call earlier."

It was time to strike out for uncharted territory . . . again. When it comes to seeking new hunting spots—something we've had to do many times over the years—Joe Elliott and I have developed a "macro-micro" approach. First we touch base with fish and game biologists or other contacts around the state to get an idea of how pheasants are faring in various locales. Once we've narrowed the search to a county or two, we hit the road and trust our own eyes and ears to identify good hunting conditions. That's when we start to employ micro techniques, which tend to be more creative and interesting. These include using the finely tuned antennae that every bird hunter develops to collect useful tidbits of information in sport shops, bars, gas stations, and cafés. The latter is where we got the tip that led us to the place we affectionately came to call "conjugal bliss."

We were sitting in a small-town café in northeastern Montana eating breakfast when the waitress stopped by to refill our coffee cups. You know the type—young, blond, friendly—a pretty, blue-eyed descendant of the Scandinavian farmers who settled the northern plains a century or so ago.

"Are you guys pheasant hunters?" she asked.

"We will be on Saturday, when the season opens," I replied.

"Lots of birds this year," she said matter-of-factly.

Our ears perked up. "We just got here and we haven't had time to look around yet."

"You know where the Lutheran church is about five miles north of here? My Uncle Fred is hauling grain, and he says the birds are conjugatin' there every morning."

Joe gulped his coffee and commenced a coughing spasm.

"Right in front of the church?" I asked.

"They're conjugatin' across the road in the grain stubble, next to the shelterbelt," she said.

The mental image of conjugating pheasants had tickled Joe's funny bone; he was starting to convulse, like a volcano fixing to blow its top. I kicked him under the table.

"Is your uncle a bird hunter?" I asked.

"Naw, he's a deacon. You know, he helps the minister pass the plate when folks all conjugate on Sunday."

I thought Joe was going to wet his pants. He quickly excused himself to go outside and check on the dogs.

"Go out and talk to my uncle about hunting—he's a mile west of the church," suggested our Nordic benefactress. "It's a big white house—mailbox says Peterson on it. He has a lot of land in Conservation Reserve."

I finished my coffee, left a generous tip and made a beeline for the truck—and the connubial promised land.

Uncle Fred turned out to be an affable sort, especially when we mentioned we'd talked to his niece. He said there'd be a few other hunters around, but most of them would avoid his recently planted Conservation Reserve land.

"Those fields are new and they're tough walking—an hour in there and you'll have leg cramps."

"Leg cramps are okay," I said, "as long as there are pheasants."

Daybreak found us on the county road waiting for shooting light. A rooster crowed in one corner of the field and two more answered. We looked at each other and smiled. Joe belled his French Brittany, Rana, and I buckled a beeper collar on my Brittany, Groucho. We knew we'd quickly lose contact with the dogs in the tall grass and weeds without a way to track them. The sun broke over the eastern horizon, casting a rosy glow on the white church steeple across the road. Time to go hunting.

We hadn't gone far when Groucho's beeper signaled he was on point. I walked in and bagged my first rooster of the season. Five minutes later Rana's bell went silent; a hen flushed, followed by a cackling rooster, which Joe dropped in the tall grass. Rana quickly found the bird and brought it to him. The next twenty minutes dissolved into a pleasant blur of dogs pointing, pheasants flushing and the smell of gunpowder on the air.

As is sometimes the case on the first day of the season, we had our three-pheasant limits all too soon. But we've learned to savor these occasional bonanzas because we know that later in the season when the roosters are scarcer and wiser we'll pay in spades for our opening day windfall.

Back at the café for lunch, we showered thanks on the lovely Brenda, with whom we were now on a first-name basis. I couldn't help thinking that if I were twenty years younger—better make it thirty—I could fall in love with more than the Montana prairie and its glorious ring-necked roosters.

On Sunday, in deference to Uncle Fred and the other folks who would be attending services at the little white church, we hunted the far end of the field. This time I uncrated my black Lab, Jenny, who takes special pleasure in burrowing under weedy tangles to boost roosters from the thick stuff. It took a bit longer than the day before, but by the time the good Lutherans had begun to gather we had extracted another limit of pheasants from Uncle Fred's field. As we were loading the dogs, Brenda drove by in her pickup truck and waved. My watch said 8:50 a.m.

That afternoon we drove forty miles north to a waterfowl management area with a mixture of upland and wetland habitat. Joe walked the grassland in search of sharp-tailed grouse while I sat in the sun on a windy pass between two ponds as teal darted past like rockets. I managed to accumulate an embarrassing collection of empty hulls in the process of bagging three bluewings and a green-wing. Joe straggled back with a couple of sharptails and complaints of birds flushing from the wrong side of the gray-green line of Russian olives a mile distant.

As you will recall from the beginning of this tale, our love affair with Uncle Fred's Conservation Reserve fields ended sadly. The winter ice storm and subsequent blizzards took a heavy toll on the pheasants throughout the region. But there are always a few survivors to form the nucleus of a new population. With a little help from Mother Nature in the way of mild winters, plus vigorous and sustained conjugation on the part of the pheasants, Joe and I knew they'd eventually return to their former abundance. In the meantime, we'd take our macro-micro show back on the road, antennae tuned to the slightest clues concerning the whereabouts of our favorite game bird.

Country Folks and City Slickers

s a lifelong pheasant hunter I've knocked on a lot of doors to
ask permission to hunt. Most of the time the response
has been a polite yes or no, and maybe a short conversation
about the weather. But once in awhile a knock on the door has introduced me to a memorable character, and sometimes it has marked
the beginning of a lasting friendship.

Down on the Yellowstone River south of Sidney a man named
August and his wife invited me in for coffee and cookies when I asked
permission to hunt. Their cozy kitchen had an old-fashioned stove
and wonderful smells emanating from the oven. We were on our
third cup of coffee and had pretty well covered the state of the world
when August's wife gave him an exasperated look and declared:
"August, can't you see this poor man wants to go hunting?" I was
younger then and itching to get after the pheasants, and apparently
my body language had begun to show it.

Many years later I read in the paper that August and his wife
had passed away and left a substantial sum of money to Montana

State University. Obviously, they could have built a McMansion to replace their humble farmhouse, but many farmers and ranchers of August's generation seemed content to live at the old home place, often the same house where they were born and raised. Their kids and grandkids don't necessarily share that notion and these days I see houses springing up in the wheat patch that would look right at home in an upscale city suburb. I can't say that I blame them, but I miss the little old houses on the prairie and the kind, generous people within.

My friends and I sometimes offer to share the game we harvest with landowners who grant us permission to hunt, but they rarely take us up on it. I think sometimes they are just being polite but some of the older folks have childhood memories of living off wild game to get through lean times. Maybe when you grow up poor and don't have anything to eat but venison and other wild game you begin to develop a fondness for beef and chicken. One rancher told me the story of his wife's family who had to go hat in hand to the local banker when she was a child to ask for an extension on their loan. They explained they would have to butcher a bull to get them through the winter. The banker, worried about his bottom line, looked at them coldly and said, "You'll go out and kill a deer to eat but by god you won't lay a hand on that bull."

Many years later, after these folks had built a successful cattle operation with an oil well or two thrown in for good measure, they could have bought and sold the flint-hearted banker. But to this day my friend's wife doesn't care much for venison.

On several occasions I've been invited to hunt pheasants with landowners and their friends or family members and for the most part it has worked out fine. But you never quite know what you're getting into when you venture afield with strangers. On one memorable hunt my boss and a co-worker and I were guided by a guy named Norbert, a big raw-boned Norwegian farmer with work-calloused hands the size of dinner plates. Norbert was in his seventies when we met him and age had slowed him a bit but he was still a bear of a man. Legend had it he had been a formidable barroom brawler in his younger days, a fact that still earned him respect in the local watering holes.

When it came time for our pheasant hunt my boss jumped in Norbert's truck, while my pal and co-worker, Mikey, rode with me. After several miles of bouncing down a rutted gravel road Norbert's truck skidded to a stop in a swirl of dust. Showing remarkable agility for a septuagenarian, Norbert bailed out, racked a shell into the chamber of his old Model 97 Winchester and cut loose at a rooster sprinting down a fencerow.

"Winged him!" yelled Norbert. "Catch him, he's gittin' away!" The sight of our boss, Speedy, who liked to lecture us on hunting ethics, racing down the fencerow in pursuit of Norbert's ground-sluiced pheasant had Mikey and me in stitches. I suppose Mikey's yelling "Fetch, Speedy, fetch!" wasn't in our best career interests, but we weren't exactly on the fast track for promotion anyway.

There was a farmhouse on the other side of the road and the young farmer who came boiling out didn't look happy. He may have had designs on that particular rooster for his Sunday dinner. Norbert met him head on and began explaining certain facts of life to him, while Speedy sheepishly retrieved Norbert's ill-gotten bird. We couldn't hear everything being said since we thought it prudent to stay in our truck and let the locals sort things out for themselves, but we did hear Norbert remind the young farmer that he hadn't even been a gleam in his mother's eye when Norbert had been getting shot at on a European battlefield during World War II.

"You'd be speakin' German right now if it wasn't for me and my buddies," declared Norbert, poking a sausage-sized index finger in the man's chest. The sight of Norbert's big hands, square jaw, and steely eyes had a calming effect on the young farmer, and with a shrug he turned around and retreated to his farmhouse, shoulders slumped, and muttering to himself.

Mikey and I debated for a time whether Norbert had actually broken any laws, and finally decided he hadn't. It's legal to carry an uncased, loaded gun in Montana, as long as there is no shell in the chamber. At the time it was legal to hunt roadside ditches, although that is no longer the case. The land wasn't posted and permission didn't seem to be an issue, since Norbert knew everyone in the county, or they knew him. But the whole episode wasn't a shining example of good hunting ethics. In our defense, we certainly hadn't seen it coming. We were just along for the ride.

Later that fall I turned into the gravel drive of a Hutterite colony near Great Falls. Hutterites are communal farmers who speak a German dialect as well as English, adhere to a strict dress code, and own all property jointly.

"You must ask Jacob about the hunting," said a woman clad in traditional dark dress and polka-dot headscarf, pointing to a nearby building. She spoke with a thick German accent. I was wearing sunglasses and as I entered the darkened building it took a moment for the scene to register. I had already blurted out "Where can I find Jacob . . ." when I noticed the room was completely quiet and that about fifty men sat silently at large dining tables, hatless, heads bowed in prayer. I had the presence of mind to remove my hat and dark glasses and bow my head while they finished praying, but I figured barging in on such a solemn moment didn't augur well for my hunting prospects.

When their prayers were finished a short, gray-bearded man approached and stared at me sternly through steel-rimmed spectacles. "Vot iss your name?" he asked. I usually introduce myself as "Dave," but for some reason I said "David."

"Dafitt. Dot iss a gut bible name," he said. "You go ahead and hunt dose birds. I hope you get a dussen of 'em." I thanked Jacob profusely and made a hasty exit. I didn't shoot "a dussen" of his roosters, but I bagged my limit of three in short order.

Then there was the man in the Missouri River Breaks who had a very large and menacing "No Trespassing" sign at the entrance to his ranch driveway. The sign noted a long list of undesirables who should not darken the man's doorstep, including salesmen, government parasites, hunters, city slickers, and college pups. I wish I could remember the whole list. This was Missouri River gumbo country, where rainy weather can render the roads impassable in a matter of a few hours.

When my two friends, college pups and city slickers of the first water, slid off a gumbo road into the ditch, they found themselves hopelessly mired not far from the ranch house of the man with the sign. This is lonely country and there was no one else for miles to turn to for help, so my friends had to screw up their courage and knock on the man's door. To their amazement, David turned out to be a friendly fellow who seemed mildly amused by my friends' predicament. He pulled them out of the ditch with his tractor and refused their offer of payment.

Down Otter Creek way I met a man named Charles, who lived in a beautiful old log ranch house out in the middle of nowhere. This guy had lots of pheasants in his creek bottom and I couldn't help but notice the two dozen fat mallards swimming in a nearby beaver pond. Charles was a thoughtful, intelligent man whose wife had passed away and whose children were grown and gone, and he was obviously starved for conversation. A presidential election was close at hand and our discussion naturally turned to politics.

I had driven a long way and I didn't want to say the wrong thing, but Charles wasn't giving me any clues about which candidate he favored in the election. Most Montana cattle ranchers are politically conservative and lean toward the Republican Party, but with wheat farmers you never can tell. To confound matters further, lots of Montana landowners have varied holdings with cattle, hay, and grain. I did some tap-dancing and seemed to be getting through the political quagmire without causing offense. I breathed a sigh of relief when Charles said, "Sure, you can hunt my birds. I've got too darned many of 'em, and I'm afraid they'll catch a disease and have a die-off. How many can you shoot?"

I said by law I could only shoot three. I stood in one place at the edge of a cattail patch and shot my limit of roosters, then watched while my black Lab flushed a dozen more. I left his place with three roosters and four nice mallards, but Charles seemed genuinely disappointed that I hadn't reduced his pheasant population to a healthier level. Or maybe he'd been looking forward to a good political argument and was put off by my namby-pamby approach to political debate.

Years ago, before the advent of computers, cell phones, and satellite TV, some country folks did indeed live isolated and simple lives. But anyone who thinks that rural people today are unsophisticated rubes is in for a big surprise—many of the farmers and ranchers I know have college degrees in things like agronomy or range science and all of them have an excellent grasp of economics, commodity prices, and modern agricultural techniques. They are computer-savvy business people who regularly make financial decisions that would give corporate executives pause for thought. Gambling on the weather and deciding when to buy fertilizer, fuel, and machinery, what and when to plant and when to harvest, and when to sell crops, cattle, or other products takes knowledge, experience, and a shrewd sense of timing.

In addition to possessing business acumen, farmers and ranchers also need to be good mechanics, veterinarians, electricians, plumbers, and carpenters. When one of my hunting partners, Buck the Whiner, locked his keys in the truck at the end of a trail a mile from a rancher friend's house, he commenced a moaning that could have been heard in the nearest town seven miles distant. He morosely pondered his options and had finally settled on throwing a rock through the window when someone wisely suggested, "Wait a minute, let's see if Jon is around before you do that."

Jon Bolstad raises Angus cattle and grows wheat and other crops on his ranch near Medicine Lake in northeastern Montana. We found him loading bales not far away and asked him if he had any ideas on getting into Buck's locked truck. To make a long story short, Jon unraveled a piece of barbed wire and opened Buck's truck in about ten minutes, and he doesn't even do that sort of thing for a living. We didn't ask him where he learned that skill but it did come to light that he'd had some formal training in car body repair as a young man. "When you make your living ranching and the nearest town of any size is thirty miles away," said Jon, "you learn to fix things and build things or you don't last long."

My friend Penny is a country girl, born and raised on a farm in eastern Montana. She is a go-getter, resourceful and smart, a hard-working entrepreneur in a small town where moneymaking opportunities are in short supply. She has assembled a half-dozen or so apartment units with kitchen facilities and a small RV park, and when pheasant season rolls around Penny's place is humming with activity. Her apartments may be modest by big-city standards, but they are clean, well-stocked with dishes and cooking utensils, comfortable, and reasonably priced.

A few years back she booked some hunters from a Midwestern city for opening week of the pheasant season. "They seemed like honest guys," she said, "so I didn't ask for a deposit." In the small town where Penny resides, people tend to keep their word and no one worries much about locking a house or vehicle. The hunters showed up the night before hunting season, noted the lack of cable TV, and said they wanted to look around a bit before committing to the rental. When Penny pointed out that they'd verbally agreed to rent her apartment unit and she had turned down several parties in the interim, they shrugged. "This ain't no #@$# Hilton," snorted one, and away they went.

Of course, there are no available motel rooms within eighty miles of the town in question on the opening weekend of pheasant season, something the city boys had failed to take into account. A few hours later they were back at Penny's place, apologizing in a most respectful tone of voice. In the meantime, Penny had rented the unit to the next group of hunters who knocked on her door. The city slickers then asked if they could park their vehicles at Penny's RV park and sleep in their trucks. She agreed, but drove a hard bargain on the price, charging them close to what they would have paid for the apartment rental in the first place. So, of course, to those of us who stay there often, Penny's place will always be known as "The #@$# Hilton."

I guess I've reached the age where pheasant hunting isn't just about pheasants anymore—it's about people and places and being in pheasant country during a beautiful time of year. Getting to know the local folks is a large part of what makes it so much fun. We need to keep in mind that hunters, farmers, and ranchers are all in this thing together—the fate of our wildlife has always hinged on cooperation and goodwill of landowners, and it always will.

So, city slickers, next time you're out in pheasant country, give a farmer or rancher a big hug. Or on second thought, just shake his hand and give him your heartfelt thanks.

The Hi-Line

The Milk River originates in Glacier National Park and meanders eastward, partly in Canada and partly in northern Montana, about 700 miles to its confluence with the Missouri River north of Fort Peck Reservoir. On his way west with the Voyage of Discovery in 1805, Meriwether Lewis named the river for its "peculiar whiteness, being about the color of a cup of tea with the admixture of a tablespoonful of milk." For much of its path the Milk parallels what Montanans call the Hi-Line, the east-west route of U.S. Highway 2 and James J. Hill's Great Northern Railway, now the Burlington-Northern line.

Last October, as Joe Elliott and I drove east on Highway 2 to hunt pheasants on a ranch where we've had success over the years, cottonwoods lit the Milk River bottom in shades of gold. East of the railroad town of Havre, once known as Bull Hook Siding, the Hi-Line towns rolled by, little burgs with names like Chinook, Zurich, Harlem, Dodson, Malta, and Saco. The warm sun on our faces, we cruised past grain elevators, gas stations, and small-town cafés. Traffic was light, mostly farmers hauling hay or poking along with their farm machinery. They gave us friendly waves as we pulled around to pass.

That evening we stopped at the ranch headquarters to ask permission to hunt, and the next morning we pulled up to a Conservation Reserve field and uncased our shotguns. The ranch has a combination of grassland and irrigated cropland sown to wheat, alfalfa, and corn, all bisected by several miles of Milk River bottom. Most hunters, given the choice of hunting the open fields or the riverbank tangles, opt for the former; Joe and I were no different. But the pheasant season had been open for a week and hunting pressure had been heavy. Most of the roosters had retreated to the wooded river bottom where they could elude hunters by slipping across the river to safety.

After working the fields for two hours with our Brittanys, Ollie and Gret, we had only one bird each to show for our efforts. We held a brief war council. "Longspur's Lair?" asked Joe, glancing toward the river bottom.

"I guess it's time to cowboy up," I sighed. We'd hunted the gnarly stretch of river bottom we call Longspur's Lair several times in previous years, and had always seen, or at least heard, roosters there. Walking is tough and shooting even tougher because of a profusion of cottonwood, Russian olive, buffaloberry, hawthorn, and wild rose. It's the kind of place where a canny rooster can survive to a ripe old age.

We kenneled the Britts and took my black Lab, Jenny, since Longspur's Lair is a place only a Labrador could love: brushy tangles, a river to swim in, and plenty of pheasant scent. Joe seemed unusually chipper for a man about to enter pheasant hunting purgatory. "The harder the hunting," he said, "the more fun we'll have. Let's flip a coin to see who walks closest to the river."

I lost the coin toss and had to walk next to the water where the brush is thickest. We hadn't gone 100 yards when Jenny struck a hot trail and nosed a rooster from a buffaloberry thicket. I dodged to the left for a better look, tripped on a root and banged my knee. The rooster cackled profanities as he sailed away unscathed. Score one for the pheasants.

The next bird got up well ahead of us and made a clean getaway. The third bird wasn't as lucky. It, too, flushed behind a screen of brush but gave me an opening as it flew over the water. When I pulled the trigger it dropped mid-river with a splash. Jenny hadn't seen it fall, so I scrambled down the steep bank to a place where I could give her a line. Then I slipped in the gooey shoreline mud and ended up calf-deep in the river. The cold water seeping over the tops of my boots gave me a case of St. Vitus' dance, and I slipped again and fell on my butt. By now the bird had floated downstream around a bend, so I had to bushwhack down the bank to catch up. Luckily the current is slow in this part of the Milk and the bird hadn't gone far. Jenny quickly swam out to get the soggy bird.

An hour later, after several more fruitless flushes, a young rooster angled back in Joe's direction, and he sent it tumbling into a patch of snowberry. We held another war council and decided to leave the field of battle to the remaining ringnecks. We clawed our way out of Longspur's Lair soaked with sweat and punctured by thorns, but we each had the satisfying heft of a rooster in our hunting vest. Jenny

the Lab, her coat caked with mud but still wagging her tail with joy, reluctantly followed.

The next morning we headed south on a gravel road through a checkerboard of sagebrush, golden wheat stubble, and grasslands baked khaki by the sun. Eventually we turned west toward a range of reddish hills, climbed slowly onto a prairie plateau and stopped at a barbed wire gate. When we got out, the pungent aroma of sagebrush filled our nostrils. We opened the gate, drove through and closed it behind us. Public land. Sharptail heaven.

We turned out the Brittanys, grabbed vests, shells, water bottles, and guns, and headed into the sagebrush. Keyed up from the drive, the dogs raced hell-bent toward the horizon while we tooted on our whistles trying to keep them from leaving the country. Far ahead, Ollie screeched to a halt. When I walked up I could see a large bird crouched in the grass in front of him.

While I pondered the situation, six sage grouse took my indecision as their cue to climb skyward. I picked a bird and toppled it into the sage. I could have shot again, but we had come here to hunt sharp-tails. I figured one sage grouse would be enough to let Ollie know I appreciated his staunch point.

Joe followed a fenceline bordering a cut wheat field while I dropped into a chokecherry draw that led down to a small reservoir. When I heard him shoot twice, I looked in his direction to see a dozen sharptails flapping and sailing toward me. They offered a crossing shot as they passed thirty yards ahead of me and twenty yards high. I swung hard, pulled ahead of the nearest bird and slapped the trigger. He slanted down and Ollie soon had him in tow.

Farther down the draw toward the reservoir Ollie pointed tentatively at the edge of the chokecherries. A grouse clucked out of the bushes, offering an easy shot. Three others flushed out of range up ahead. I heard Joe shoot two more times as he worked his way toward us. When we met at the reservoir to let the dogs get a drink and cool off in the water, he was smiling ear to ear. "Gret made two great points," he said, pulling three sharptails from his vest. "I doubled on the first one." After a rest we made a wide circle back to the trucks, bagging a sharptail apiece along the way.

That afternoon we visited an abandoned homestead near the Milk River, one of many such places along the Hi-Line slowly crumbling back to the prairie sod. Sadly, each year there are fewer of these dilapidated buildings standing, as they become victims of demolition, fire, or the ravages of time, wind, and weather. Perhaps some landowners view them as eyesores, or decide the land can be put to more profitable use. The farmers who once lived in these structures have long since passed from the scene.

Years ago we named this one "Wagon Wheel" in honor of a wooden-spoked wheel that leans against a weathered wall of the old house. We have often surprised a covey of Huns loafing in the shelterbelt that protects the adjoining farmyard, or a pheasant resting in the tall weeds growing up inside an old corral. I like to think of it as a happy place, where children once played in a sunlit yard and hot apple pies sat cooling on the windowsill. But it just as easily could have been a place of broken dreams, where a struggling family saw their hopes evaporate in a cloud of Depression-era dust. Once I saw a great horned owl resting on the ledge of a glassless window. As I watched, he closed one eye and then the other, as if winking at me; perhaps he knew the story, but he wasn't about to tell.

As Joe walked the shelterbelt with Gret, I checked out the corral. When Ollie's bell fell silent near the fence, the hair stood up on the back of my neck. A loose piece of tin on a shed roof twanged in the breeze, heightening the tension. Once I saw a rattlesnake disappear down a badger hole nearby; although October is a little late for rattlesnakes in Montana, on a warm day you never know.

As I approached, Ollie rolled his eyes toward me with a conspiratorial glance. "Whoa," I said softly, more to steady my nerves than his. I tried peering into the grass. "Got a bird for me?" Like the great horned owl, Ollie knew, but he wasn't talking.

I took one more step and a rooster pheasant clattered skyward, his plumage glowing bronze in the October sun. For a moment he hung there, suspended against a cobalt sky sprinkled with fleecy clouds, then leveled off and shifted into overdrive. My load of No. 6 caught up with him before he could make good his escape.

As Joe and I sat by the wagon wheel that day sharing our sandwiches with Gret and Ollie, I wondered aloud if the people who once lived here had been pheasant hunters. Pheasants were well established in Montana by the 1930s, and by 1940 the pheasant had become the most popular game bird in the state. I like to think there had been pheasants hanging in the shade to feed a hungry farm family many years before we wandered onto the scene.

New Englanders have coverts like the Old Stone Wall, Alder Jungle, or Drummer's Log—names that conjure up an image of autumn hardwoods, a Belton setter, and pipe smoke on the breeze. Those are all good things.

Montanans have the Hi-Line, with its abandoned homesteads, Milk River tangles, wind-scrubbed prairie, and immense sky. Those, too, are very good things.

Sundown Roosters

———◆◈◆———

If I had to choose one hour of the day to hunt pheasants with a dog, I'd take the last hour. Birds are active then—filling their crops, picking grit, and moving toward roosting areas where they'll settle in for the night. As the air cools, scenting conditions are often the best they've been all day. The air takes on a heavier, almost palpable feel. Sometimes it almost seems like I can smell the birds myself.

Besides, it's a beautiful time to be afield. The light softens and the autumn sky ignites in shades of orange, pink, or lavender as the sun drops toward the horizon. Best of all, I don't have much competition. Many hunters have already filled their limits. Others have retired to camp or motel for a cold beer and a hot dinner. And some are just plain tuckered out and have packed it in for the day. So it's just me and my dog out there, locked in a sundown chess match with a wily rooster.

Does that mean I'll pass up a morning limit of pheasants if given the chance? Nope. I'm not crazy. Pheasant hunting can be fickle, and wise hunters take the opportunities as they come. But early in the season if the weather is warm I'd rather hunt for a few hours in the morning, rest during the middle of the day, and venture out again in the cool of the evening. Later in the season, I often don't have a choice. Days are shorter and pheasants harder to come by. Late afternoon often finds me lacking a bird or two of a three-bird limit.

Such was the case one November when Buck MacLaurin, Joe Elliott, and I pondered our chances of finding a late-day rooster in a northern Montana Conservation Reserve field. We had hunted most of the day with precious little to show for it. We hadn't hunted this field before so we took off with our dogs in different directions to scout it out. I hadn't gone far when I started seeing pheasant roosts in the heavy grass and alfalfa undergrowth. But after combing the field for an hour with my Brittany, Ollie, it became clear the birds simply weren't there. The weather had been unseasonably mild, there was no snow, and plenty of hunters had worked the area. Footsore and discouraged, I returned to the truck, swapped my hunting boots for sneakers, and sat on the tailgate with Ollie while I waited for Buck and Joe.

As the sun moved closer to the horizon, a rooster crowed several hundred yards away on the far side of a hill. Ollie perked up his ears. Then another rooster answered. Trouble is, these birds weren't in the Conservation Reserve tract—they were in the middle of a big wheat stubble field that extended east for a half-mile. That solved the mystery of why I hadn't found birds in the Conservation Reserve— the warm weather had allowed them to hang out in the stubble where they could see and hear hunters approaching from any direction. They were daring me to put my boots on and come after them. So I reluctantly obliged, figuring the thin cover would make it a futile effort.

I walked into the stubble and released Ollie, who raced to the top of the hill a hundred yards ahead, looking for Loudmouth No. 1. By the time I trudged up there, Ollie had been on point several minutes. But the rooster wasn't about to let me get within shooting range; he cackled his way out of the stubble, taking three hens with him. Undaunted, Ollie raced over the next hill in search of Loudmouth No. 2.

When I topped the crest there stood Ollie, patiently pointing again. This bird flushed at about fifty yards but made a fatal mistake. He came ten yards closer as he angled back toward the Conservation Reserve field, offering me a crossing shot. I don't like taking forty-yard shots at late-season ringnecks, but this time the odds were in my favor. His profile was exposed and when I knocked him down he had nowhere to hide. Ollie scooped him up and delivered him to me.

That's not the first time I've been alerted to a rooster's presence by its crowing, although I hear it more often in the morning than in the afternoon. The sound has a ventriloquial quality that makes it hard to pin down, but if I get a fix on the location I always check it out. My stubble field experience notwithstanding, the noise usually comes from heavier cover where birds are less inclined to flush wild or take off running late in the day.

While using your ears can give you a heads up on a rooster's presence, more often your eyes will tip you off to a spot worth hunting. Birds are typically moving from feeding or loafing areas to heavier roosting cover in late afternoon and sometimes they fly from grain fields to shelterbelts, brushy draws, cattails, or dense Conservation Reserve fields. Marking them down will at least give you a place to start.

With my usual bad timing I twisted my knee a few years back and had to play couch potato for a week right in the heart of the pheasant season. Finally I couldn't stand it anymore and decided to try an afternoon hunt in a Conservation Reserve field that has yielded a rooster or two for me in recent years. As luck would have it, Ollie pinned a rooster not far from the truck and I bagged the bird. I tried hunting a while longer but the uneven ground and thick grass had my knee joint clicking like a castanet, so I decided to call it a day. As I drove home past Freezeout Lake Wildlife Management Area west of Great Falls about 4 p.m., I saw a rooster fly across the road and disappear over a hill. My knee instantly felt better. I quickly found a place to park, uncrated my black Lab, Jenny, and crossed the fence into the public hunting area.

Once I cleared the rise I could see a patch of cattails surrounded by knee-high grass and weeds that hadn't been visible from the road; it was just the right size for a gimpy hunter and an old Lab to cover in a half-hour. But I hadn't been in the cover ten minutes when Jenny's tail began gyrating wildly—always a sign that good things are about to happen—and a minute later she boosted a rooster from the cattails twenty yards in front of me. The shot should have been an easy one, but just as I pulled the trigger a gust of wind gave the bird a rocket-fuel boost. The rooster came down wing-tipped but Jenny had it in her jaws before it could get up and running.

Another twinge in my knee told me I was done hunting but I still had a half-hour to enjoy the "crepuscular bonus" of a late afternoon outing. Many wildlife species are most active during the twilight hours of dusk and dawn—biologists refer to them as crepuscular. Even if pheasant finding is slow, there is often a white-tailed deer in an alfalfa field, a red fox trotting down a distant fenceline, or a flock of ducks or geese overhead to admire. Freezeout Lake plays host to a fantastic migration of tundra swans, snow geese, and other waterfowl each spring and fall. The snow-white, long-necked swans were flying low that afternoon, bucking a strong west wind. I love watching waterfowl and I spent the remaining daylight with a pair of binoculars as restless flocks of swans, geese, and ducks traded from fields to marsh until a blood-red sun slid behind the Rocky Mountain Front.

Does going the extra mile before dark always pay off? No. There have been plenty of times when all I got from my last hour of hunting was tired legs. But there is something satisfying about giving the day full measure. As Izaak Walton said of fishing, "You must indure worst luck sometime, or you will never make a good angler." He could just as well have been talking about pheasant hunting. Even if I don't get my sundown rooster, dinner tastes better when I straggle in at dark knowing I gave it my best shot.

My old Brittany, Groucho, who went on to the great Conservation Reserve field in the sky a few years back, knew something about never-say-die pheasant hunting. Several friends and I were on a four-day hunting expedition in southwestern North Dakota. Our host had promised us great pheasant hunting in his corn and sunflower fields, and he wasn't kidding. We saw literally hundreds of pheasants and easily bagged our possession limits. But hunting them involved walking the fields with a line of hunters and driving the birds over blockers. Our retrievers had a field day gathering up birds, while our pointing dogs languished in their crates. Our farmer friend didn't have much land in Conservation Reserve, and the grassy fields adjoining his corn and sunflowers belonged to other landowners. One of these fields, in particular, made our mouths water, since we knew it held hundreds of birds.

Apparently fourteen-year-old Groucho knew it too. Late in the afternoon on the last day of our hunt I made the mistake of letting him out of the truck at the edge of this field for a quick leg-lifting while we loaded our gear prior to heading back to the farmhouse. I took my eyes off him for a minute and when I turned around he was already fifty yards out in the Conservation Reserve field. The field was posted "no trespassing" so now I had a moral dilemma. Groucho was quite deaf, so yelling and whistling had no effect. He had no intention of coming back anyway.

Soon he was eighty yards away, pointing a pheasant. While I deliberated, the bird flew, and Groucho was on to another one . . . and another one . . . and another one. I couldn't see him anymore, but I could trace his progress by the birds boiling out of the field. Besides being deaf, Groucho was on his last legs physically. His breathing had gradually gotten so labored that any exertion caused him distress— my vet had pointed out several suspicious masses on X-rays taken earlier in the year—cancerous tumors, likely. Sundown wasn't far off and he was still headed directly away from me, so I grabbed a leash and took off after him. I figured any landowner with an ounce of compassion would cut me some slack if I explained I was trying to retrieve an old warrior who had temporarily lost his mind.

The field was a hunter's dream, thickly vegetated with gnarly clumps of alfalfa and rank weeds, but a nightmare for a tired soul trying to jog after a pheasant-crazed Brittany. Soon I was having breathing problems of my own. About the time I was ready to give up I caught sight of him—on point, eighty yards ahead in a thin spot in the cover. I prayed for the bird to hold while I thrashed and stumbled my way to him and got him on the leash. Once he realized the game was over he flopped down on the ground, sides heaving, gasping for air like a marathon runner at the finish line.

By the time I got back to the truck with Groucho, my "friends" were having a tailgate party, complete with cold beverages and snacks. There was great hooting, applauding, and snickering at "Dave and Groucho's excellent adventure." You get the picture. Enough time has passed that I can now see the humor in that sundown pheasant hunt, but it took awhile.

Old Groucho, bless his hunter's heart, survived the outing, and lived to point a covey of Huns later in the fall—his last covey, as it turned out. That November he died in his sleep in northeastern Montana during a pheasant-hunting trip, and I buried him on a hill overlooking a lovely lake. I know that over the course of the year a pheasant or two will wander near the big rock that marks his grave, and the thought of it makes me smile. I sit there at least once each autumn watching the ducks fly back and forth across the lake, and if I wait until sunset invariably I hear a rooster crow.

While I'm there I reflect on a pursuit that teaches us all a little something about work and fun, success and failure, and, at least where old dogs are concerned, tears and laughter. You can't help but respect this bird that sometimes frustrates and bedevils us, and admire his beauty, his wariness, and his toughness. One thing is certain: bagging a sundown rooster is a perfect way to end the day.

www.ingramcontent.com/pod-product-compliance
Lightning Source LLC
Chambersburg PA
CBHW061018280326
41935CB00009B/1010